'Incisive, stimulating and highly readable. Peter Ricketts turns forty years' experience of British foreign policymaking into a road map of where Britain should be heading in the post-Brexit, post-Covid world.'

Professor David Reynolds, author of
Island Stories: An Unconventional Hi[story]

'Peter Ricketts has used his experie[nce] [as one of] the best diplomats of his generation to produce a book that is magisterial in its scope and analysis. Essential reading for all who care about Britain's position in the world.'

Jack Straw, former Foreign Secretary

'A sharp and salutary reality check from one of Britain's wisest and most experienced diplomats.'

Andrew Adonis, author of *Ernest Bevin: Labour's Churchill*

'Sharp and engaging... All of us who care about Britain remaining a major force in shaping the international order should pay careful attention to both the analysis and policy recommendations of *Hard Choices*.'

**Kori Schake, Director of Foreign and Defense
Policy at the American Enterprise Institute**

'A candid and sometimes brutal sizing up of past mistakes, of chances missed and of opportunities still open.'

Sir David Omand, former Director of GCHQ

'No one is more able than Peter Ricketts to set out clearly and sensibly the parameters of Britain's strategy in the age of Brexit, climate change and threats from China.'

Chris Patten, former Governor of Hong Kong

Peter Ricketts has been at the heart of Britain's foreign policy for more than forty years. He was Chairman of the Joint Intelligence Committee, UK Permanent Representative to NATO, Permanent Secretary in the Foreign Office, National Security Adviser and Ambassador to France. He has written for the *FT*, *The Times*, the *New Statesman* and *Prospect*, and regularly appears on Sky News and the BBC. He is a member of the House of Lords.

HARD CHOICES

The Making and Unmaking of Global Britain

PETER RICKETTS

Atlantic Books
London

Published in hardback in Great Britain in 2021 by Atlantic Books, an imprint of Atlantic Books Ltd.

This paperback edition published in 2022.

10 9 8 7 6 5 4 3 2

A CIP catalogue record for this book is available from the British Library.

Paperback ISBN: 978 1 83895 183 2
E-book ISBN: 978 1 83895 182 5

Design and typesetting benstudios.co.uk

Printed and bound by CPI Group (UK) Ltd, Croydon CR0 4YY

Atlantic Books
An imprint of Atlantic Books Ltd
Ormond House
26–27 Boswell Street
London
WC1N 3JZ

www.atlantic-books.co.uk

CONTENTS

PREFACE TO THE PAPERBACK EDITION

'Where was Global Britain on the streets of Kabul?' asked Theresa May during an angry debate in the House of Commons on 18 August 2021 after the chaotic evacuation of Western military forces from Afghanistan. The question homed in with deadly accuracy on the central weakness of Britain's foreign policy – the yawning gap between the delusions of grandeur harboured by the government and the hard realities of Britain's diminished role in the world.

President Biden's handling of the withdrawal from Afghanistan revealed much about his real priorities. After the damage done by Trump in walking away from America's international commitments while cosying up to authoritarians like Putin, the new President's 'America is back' mantra was greeted with something close to euphoria in Western capitals. He moved quickly to take the US back into the UN climate process and to restore a cooperative tone in dealings with NATO and the EU. In all the excitement, it was easy to forget that Biden's primary focus was on showing his divided nation that he was relentlessly pursuing US interests. His commitment to end the 'forever war' in Afghanistan was popular domestically. He therefore pressed ahead with the rapid withdrawal of US forces, paying no attention to the views of America's allies. Their loyalty and sacrifice through 20 years of shared military operations in Afghanistan counted for nothing.

This was particularly galling for the Johnson government. The UK had been the second largest troop contributor in Afghanistan and had taken the second highest number of combat deaths. To make matters worse, the case for Brexit had rested heavily on the assumption that, freed from the shackles of the EU, Britain would return to a central role in world affairs by leveraging its privileged relationship with Washington. But the high hopes had been disappointed. Biden showed no interest in a US-UK trade deal. The events in Kabul made embarrassingly clear how dependent Britain was on the US, and how little real influence it had on the big decisions in Washington.

A few weeks later, Australia, the US and UK announced a new security partnership. The timing could not have been better for the battered Johnson government. The new AUKUS pact, based on the sale to Australia of nuclear-powered submarines of the kind operated by the US and UK, was a presentational godsend for London. It provided welcome reassurance that Britain still counted in Washington, and gave some substance to the vacuous 'Global Britain' concept. But whether taking on this new security commitment is really in Britain's longer-term interests is much less clear. If competition turned into conflict in Asia, would Britain be in a position to make much contribution, even if there was public support for doing so?

The strategic benefits were much more compelling for the other two participants. Australia had decided that the growing Chinese military threat made it necessary to buy the most capable submarines on the planet. For the US, the new partnership tied two close allies more tightly into a network of power in the Indo-Pacific. In the process, the three countries shouldered the French unceremoniously out of an earlier deal to supply Australia with diesel-engined submarines. That was to have been the centrepiece of a new partnership which President Macron was building with Australia, as a contribution to Western engagement in the Indo-

Pacific region. The AUKUS deal left this policy in ruins and the French feeling betrayed. It inevitably led them to question the value of NATO if this was how their allies treated them.

The thread running through these two episodes was Biden's single-minded focus on strengthening America's position for the looming confrontation with China, and his willingness to ride roughshod over the interests of his allies in the process. This has reinforced the conviction in Europe that Washington has become an unpredictable partner who can no longer be relied on to take account of Europe's security interests. It has therefore given new impetus to the French-led drive to increase Europe's strategic autonomy. Support for the idea of a greater European capacity to act independently of the Americans is even beginning to be heard on the right of British politics. Tom Tugendhat, the Chairman of the Commons' Foreign Affairs Committee, in the best speech of the August 2021 Afghanistan debate, called for a 'vision, clearly articulated, for reinvigorating our European NATO partners to make sure we are not dependent on a single ally, on the decision of a single leader'.

The idea that European countries could replace what the US provides for the defence of Europe is fanciful in anything other than the very long term. But Biden's unilateralism, coming after Trump's destructiveness, has given European nations a new incentive to equip themselves to stand on their own feet in terms of military operations short of a major war. Britain should be involved in helping shape that important debate. The problem is that this is taking place not in NATO, but in the EU. The Johnson government's ideological opposition to any cooperation with the EU in this area leaves Britain unable to influence thinking in an area which could have significant implications for our security.

I began to write this book because I was convinced that Britain faced some profoundly important choices about its role and priorities in a world where the familiar system of international rules was breaking down fast. Since I finished writing less than a year ago, it has become even more obvious that Britain is in urgent need of a new national strategy. My hope that the pandemic might lead to a new surge of international cooperation has not been borne out so far – the world has settled back all too quickly into the old rivalries. The British Government's Integrated Review of Security, Defence Development and Foreign Policy, published in March 2021, gave a compelling analysis of global trends and the challenges these presented. But on what Britain should do next, the Review fell into the trap outlined in Chapter 6. It assembled an impressive list of ambitions, but failed to set any priorities. It pledged, for example, that Britain would be a soft power superpower, a science and technology superpower by 2030, the leading defence power in Europe, as well as at the forefront of cyber technology and of combating climate change. In terms of geographical focus, the review promised a tilt to the Indo-Pacific, but also more engagement in Africa and the Middle East. There were some references to cooperating with individual European countries, but the EU was largely airbrushed out. Throughout the Review, measured official prose rubbed shoulders with grandiose claims, for example that Britain would be a global power 'moving the dial on international issues of consequence' and 'shaping the international order of the future'. This flag-waving exceptionalism was left looking distinctly threadbare by what happened in Kabul.

The art of strategy is about making choices. The Integrated Review gave no clear sense of what the government actually plans to do. Indeed it left the suspicion that there is no real strategy, beyond setting out bold aspirations in all directions and then continuing to muddle through. That impression was borne out when some of the Integrated Review's aspirations were immediately undermined by the government's own actions. Having proclaimed, for example, that Britain was a soft power superpower and a force for good in the world, ministers then cut the aid budget by 40% in the middle of the pandemic. The G7 summit which the UK chaired in June 2021 was a golden opportunity to show what Britain could achieve at the centre of global diplomacy. The agenda covered weighty issues such as preparing for the Glasgow climate summit later in the year, and helping poorer nations recover from the pandemic. But the prime minister put most of his energy into a public spat with President Macron about the impact of the UK/EU Northern Ireland Protocol on the supply of chilled sausages to Northern Ireland. In a similar way, the Glasgow summit then took place against the background of a furious UK-French row over fishing rights around the Channel Islands. As long as Britain's relationship with its European neighbours remains dysfunctional, this will keep getting in the way of London's efforts to show global leadership.

The sun-filled Cornwall summit was also the setting for the first substantive meeting between Biden and Johnson. The British side seized on the opportunity to mobilise a piece of history on behalf of a prime minister who loves to see himself in Churchillian terms. They decided to propose a New Atlantic Charter, exploiting the fact that the date of the Cornwall summit fell close to the 80th anniversary of the first wartime US/UK summit in August 1941 which produced the original Atlantic Charter. The story of that remarkable document and its influence is recounted in Chapter 1, and I was intrigued to see how the 2021 version would match up to its illustrious predecessor.

The Johnson-Biden document re-commits the two countries to promoting shared values, supporting the rules-based international order and fulfilling their common responsibilities for maintaining security, international stability and resilience. It pledges that 'our NATO allies and partners will always be able to count on us' (this point seemed to have slipped Biden's mind when it came to the Afghanistan pull-out two months later). However, the New Atlantic Charter also underlines inadvertently how much British influence has diminished over the last 80 years. In 1941, Winston Churchill and Franklin D. Roosevelt each persuaded the other to make difficult compromises. By finding new areas of common ground, they paved the way for the great post-war institutions such as the UN. The 2021 Charter broke no new ground and opened up no new paths to the future. It was a clever re-packaging of existing positions to serve an immediate public relations need, but it will not affect the course of international relations.

The hard choices for Britain set out in the closing chapters of the book are, if anything, getting starker. The evacuation from Kabul brings down the curtain on three decades of Western efforts to make the world a safer place by using military force to intervene in other people's conflicts. There will be no more expeditionary operations involving Western boots on the ground for the foreseeable future. But the dilemma remains that not intervening also has consequences. It allows other powers with very different ideas about human rights and the rule of law to expand their spheres of influence, as China is now doing in Afghanistan. It leaves the wealthy democracies vulnerable to all the effects of state collapse, from refugee flows to safe spaces for terrorists to operate. Britain has much to contribute to international efforts to tackle the world's problems, but to do so it needs to identify a few priorities and pursue them ruthlessly.

One of the book's main themes is that democracies have lost the art of strategic thinking, and that Britain is suffering from a particularly acute case of this affliction. The difference between the two Atlantic Charters is a measure of the decline. Among the examples of powerful strategic thinking from an earlier era which I examine in Chapter 5 is the 1960 Future Policy Study. This was commissioned by Harold Macmillan to frame a new national strategy after the humiliation of Suez in 1956. Its starkest warning was that Britain should never find itself having to make a final choice between the US and Europe. The authors warned that any such choice would not be compatible with our vital national interests, and would mean the destruction of the Atlantic alliance. Macmillan took their warning very seriously, and acted on it. The risk now is that a combination of the Johnson government's refusal to develop a working relationship with the EU and its opportunistic embrace of the new AUKUS pact is drawing Britain into ever closer alignment with a United States which is pulling away from Europe and its security concerns. At the same time, many European countries are losing trust in America's reliability and resolving to reduce their dependence on the US.

The transatlantic gap is widening, and Britain is seen in much of Europe as having turned its back on its neighbours. The government's pretensions to be a global power playing a key role in the Indo-Pacific are dangerously out of kilter with the reality that our economic and security interests are first and foremost in Europe. The economic and political damage done by Britain's chaotic departure from the EU is becoming ever clearer as the pandemic begins to recede. The risks of making a fateful choice between the US and Europe are as great as in 1960. The country's security and prosperity, the very unity of the United Kingdom, are at stake. Decisions taken in the years ahead will be the making or the unmaking of Global Britain.

Peter Ricketts, October 2021

INTRODUCTION

The mobile phone signal is always bad as the Eurostar train races across northern France on its way to Paris. It was no different on the morning of Saturday, 19 March 2011. But it was more than usually inconvenient. I was with Prime Minister David Cameron as his National Security Adviser and we were on our way to a summit meeting called by his friend President Nicolas Sarkozy about the crisis in Libya. The Prime Minister needed to give his final agreement, in suitably guarded language, for a British submarine to launch its Tomahawk missiles as part of a coordinated air strike on the military units of the Gaddafi regime heading to wreak revenge on opponents of his regime gathered in Benghazi. After several tense minutes, we got through on the phone, and before long we were disembarking in Europe's worst station, the Gare du Nord.

On that Saturday morning in the Elysée Palace, Sarkozy had called together representatives from the thirty or so countries which had agreed to form a broad coalition to stop Gaddafi killing his own people and, in the process, snuffing out what was still known hopefully as the Arab Spring. The international news had been dominated for months by the series of popular uprisings in North Africa, beginning in Tunisia in late 2010 and spreading to Egypt. They succeeded in dislodging long-standing dictators in both countries. It felt like a moment of hope as young people began to mobilize using social media across the Arab world to demand political and economic freedoms. Cameron was the first world leader to visit Tahrir Square in central Cairo, in the days after President Mubarak was deposed in early February 2011.

The civic-minded young protesters we met on that trip were not seeking revolution but their rights to peaceful protest and freedom of speech under the rule of law. As Cameron and I were mixing with the crowds in Cairo, we were getting reports of a popular uprising in Libya. Gaddafi – a forty-year dictator – was responding with a brutal crackdown. Memories of previous atrocities cast their shadow over decision-making in Paris and London in those early months of 2011. Cameron and Sarkozy had both been young politicians at the time of the genocide in Rwanda in 1994 and the massacre at Srebrenica in Bosnia in 1995. Both were determined to prevent a repeat in Libya. So they forced the pace of international decision-making in the face of the blood-curdling threats Gaddafi was making against his own population.

Before the full meeting in the ornate ballroom of the Elysée Palace, Sarkozy invited Cameron and Hillary Clinton, the US Secretary of State, and their advisers for a quick coffee to align positions among the three main participants. The French President, fizzing with energy as always, was in his element as the impresario of his own show. As we sat in a semi-circle around his enormous desk, Sarkozy looked at his watch and announced theatrically that the French Rafale jets were in the air to bomb the leading column of Gaddafi forces before they could reach Benghazi. He had jumped the gun. It got him a good headline – and the Rafales did indeed catch some armoured vehicles while they were still out in the desert.

The really significant moment at that pre-conference session was when Clinton asked the American Chief of Joint Operations accompanying her to set out US plans. The imposing figure of the General rose to his feet, two rows of medals glinting on his chest. He proceeded to brief the small group of us as if we were several hundred on a parade ground. But the substance of his briefing was a lot less commanding than the General himself. He spelled out the implications of what President Barack Obama had already told Cameron and Sarkozy in separate secure phone calls several nights earlier – that this was to be the opportunity for the Europeans to take the responsibility for sorting out a security crisis in their own backyard. The US would take part in air strikes for the first week but would then take a back seat, limiting their support to some specialist assets that only they could supply, such as tanker aircraft and search and rescue assistance. To make the point even clearer, Obama had decided that US military officers serving in NATO posts would play no part in the NATO operation.

As I listened to the General on that Paris morning spelling out that the US would play a secondary role in the Libya operation, I knew that this was a turning point. Obama was sending the clearest of messages about changing US security priorities. For most of the twentieth century, the Americans had seen Europe and its neighbourhood as central to their security. When the Europeans appealed for help, the US cavalry came riding over the hill to their rescue, often with a delay, but usually with decisive effect. That was true from the First World War right through to the conflicts in Bosnia and Kosovo in the 1990s. In Paris on that March morning, we learned that the global geometry of power had shifted decisively. US attention was turning to the emerging threat to their position in Asia from China. This decision to stand back from the Libya conflict was a harbinger of a fundamental strategic shift in Washington, which accelerated after Xi Jinping took the reins of power as Party Leader in 2012 and proceeded to mount a much more open bid to shoulder the US aside in East Asia.

There was another factor in play as well. Obama had been elected on a platform to get US combat forces out of Iraq. American public opinion had turned against an operation which had been a success in rapidly overturning Saddam Hussein's regime, but which had descended into a long and bitter occupation in which Western forces had become the problem rather than the solution. Obama was still in the process of winding down the US operation in Iraq in 2011. He was in no mood to get caught up in a further open-ended commitment in the Middle East and most certainly not one which would involve putting large numbers of US soldiers in harm's way.

None of the European countries were willing to put boots on the ground either. The question of deploying Western ground forces – either to defeat Gaddafi's forces, or to stabilize the situation after his regime collapsed – simply never arose. Libya marked the end of a cycle in Western thinking about how to safeguard security and protect core values. During the Cold War, NATO members spent forty years at high readiness for full-scale war. In the ten years after 1989, the US regularly dispatched its armed forces to intervene in other countries' affairs under the banner of upholding international peace and security, with enthusiastic support from the British and varying levels of support from other allies.

The experience of occupying Iraq after 2003 broke this cycle. It destroyed public confidence that the cost in lives and money produced any benefit, either for Western security or for the countries Washington and London were trying to help. The Iraq effect restricted the West's options in Libya to using economic pressure and air strikes to try to protect the civilian population. Once the regime fell, the new National Transitional Council was never able to impose its authority across the country and prevent a slide into anarchy. So the careful preparations for the aftermath – the stockpiling of immediate humanitarian aid in Tunisia and the planning for longer-term support to a new government in Tripoli – could not be put into effect. Since NATO had no forces on the ground, there was no way to prevent the slide into lawlessness and violence which made it impossible for the development agencies to get to work.

By the time of the Syrian civil war in 2013, the reluctance of Western countries to get drawn into any military involvement was even clearer. The endless conflict in Syria led to terrible suffering for the civilian population and a huge outflow of refugees to neighbouring countries and then on towards Europe. The ISIS terrorist group exploited the anarchy in much of the country to establish a base from which to export terrorism. Obama's unwillingness to play the traditional American role of crisis management in the case of Syria left the door open for President Vladimir Putin to strengthen Russia's military position in the region. President Donald Trump's sudden decision in 2019 to withdraw the residual US troop presence in Syria encouraged Turkey to invade Northern Syria, with the aim of crushing Kurdish forces which they regarded as terrorists. Wherever the US and its allies have pulled back, other powers with different agendas have filled the vacuum. Choosing to stand back from international crisis management also has consequences.

The shifting balance of economic and political power would itself have been enough over time to call into question the post-war settlement. All international institutions become obsolete sooner or later. China and India have been outperforming Western economies for decades. China is already by some measures the largest economy in the world and projections suggest that India's gross domestic product could also overtake

America's in the decade after 2030.[1] The impact of these deep trends has been magnified and speeded up by human error. The decision by President George W. Bush[2] and Prime Minister Tony Blair to invade Iraq in 2003, without a clear mandate from the Security Council, undermined the moral authority of both countries to demand that others respect the UN Charter principles. It also damaged the public's confidence in the competence of governments to make effective decisions for their security. The strangeness of the Libya operation – with the world's pre-eminent military power standing aside and watching its allies try and fail to achieve a more stable post-Gaddafi country – was the first sign of how powerful the Iraq effect would be. The aftershocks continue to ripple out in the form of violence and civil wars in the Middle East, all of which has fuelled Islamist terrorism against the West and immigration into Europe from war-torn countries. Putin has seized the opportunity to pursue a much more aggressive foreign policy, sending his forces into Georgia, Ukraine and Syria, while using new techniques such as cyber attacks to pursue old Russian tactics of subversion and disinformation against Western countries.

The loss of Western credibility in security affairs happened in the same years as confidence in the financial system was undermined by the crash of 2008. The years of austerity that followed fanned public anger against globalization and the metropolitan elites who seemed to suffer no consequences. These multiple grievances, and the striking failure of political systems in Europe and America to spot them and deal with them, opened the door to populist leaders and sent a wider signal that the Western model was running out of steam.

China under Xi Jinping was quick to exploit the opportunity by mounting a direct challenge to US political and military dominance in Asia, coupled with a bid for global leadership of key areas of future technology. The Chinese have pushed out their defensive military perimeter in the South China Sea. With their Belt and Road initiative, they are building a strategic network of ports and rail links intended to give them control of Europe–Asia trade in future decades. China does not have colonial ambitions in terms of ruling large swathes of territory, but the technique of dominating transport routes to dictate the terms of trade is one that the eighteenth-century East India Company would have recognized.

The fact that Huawei won the race to bring the latest 5G telecoms equipment to market – offering more advanced and cheaper technology than anything US or European suppliers could produce – demonstrated the boldness of the challenge from China. It also shone a spotlight on the failure of Western countries to foresee the looming threat and organize themselves to meet it. China is in the process of disproving the long-standing Western assumption that economic progress and the growth of a middle class would lead to irresistible public demands for greater freedom of choice and expression. Instead, the Chinese leadership have clamped down hard on any sign of dissent from the Party line and have turned the internet into a tool for control and surveillance of the citizen. Russia seeks to dominate its neighbourhood and to destabilize the West. Putin is good at disruption but has nothing constructive to offer in terms of international cooperation. China aims to modify, replace or ignore a system which they see as imposing the US model of democracy, open markets and respect for human rights.

The impact of the challenge from Russia and China is all the greater because the US itself is losing interest in leading the system it was instrumental in creating. The trend was already clear when Obama wanted to stand back from conflicts such as Libya and Syria and shift more responsibility onto America's allies. Trump rejected the whole idea that America had allies. In his world view, relations between countries are transactional, based on the raw politics of economic and military power to back up personal deal-making. President Joe Biden moved fast to repair America's alliances and to rejoin international negotiations on climate change and trade. But he leads a deeply polarized nation beset by domestic problems. For all his Atlanticism, he is likely to continue on the course set by Obama of reducing over time the American contribution to European security.

That has major implications for America's allies in NATO. For the first time since the Cold War, they are facing state-based threats. Preoccupied by interventions in what Blair called 'other people's conflicts'[3] and by the threat from Islamist terrorism, Britain and other Western nations were caught off guard by the sudden shift in the strategic landscape and now find themselves poorly prepared to deal with it. They did not give enough collective attention to the mounting challenge from China and Russia.

Now, the world is changing faster than governments can adapt their policies or publics their long-settled assumptions. To make matters worse, Western governments have lost the art of strategic thinking. Governing in a democracy under the brutal pressures of the 24/7 media, amplified by the incessant drumbeat of social media, has become a continuous round of crisis management and campaigning. The demand for instant response to breaking news has raised the political tempo to the point where decisions are often rushed and ill thought-out. Ministers live in the chaos of the moment, with no time to pause and think about the longer-term consequences of their decisions. Recent British history could have been very different if Blair had taken the time for a strategic review before committing to George W. Bush in 2002 to be with him in Iraq come what may, or if Cameron had done the same before calling a referendum on Britain's membership of the EU. Britain would have been better prepared for Covid-19 if the government had acted on the clear warnings in the 2010 and 2015 National Security Strategies about the risk of just such a pandemic.

Muddling through and making incremental changes on the basis of a few settled principles mostly worked well for Western democracies under the protective bubble of American leadership. But major disruptions make it essential to rethink the fundamentals of national strategy. This is one of those periods, as significant as the years after 1945, particularly for Britain. The decision to leave the EU was both a symptom and a cause of the wider upheaval, and leaves the country facing a series of difficult decisions. Outside the EU, Britain is more dependent on its strategic partnership with the US, but less useful to Washington given its lack of leverage in Europe. Its foreign policy will necessarily be heavily weighted towards securing trade deals. This mercantilism will mean a difficult balancing act between commercial interests and pursuing a values-based foreign policy standing up for democracy and human rights. Countries such as China and Saudi Arabia will not hesitate to use Britain's need for export contracts and investment to press for criticism of their wider policies to be muted.

Life outside the EU is full of risks for Britain. But it does at least create the opportunity to come to grips at last with the uncomfortable truth that the country's image of itself is significantly out of kilter with reality. Winston Churchill's dream of sustaining a British place in the 'Big Three' with the US and

Soviet Union was unrealistic in 1945 and evaporated with the onset of the Cold War. But Britain *did* leverage its prestige at the end of the war to play an outsize role in the design of the post-war international order. In the process, it ensured for itself the trappings of a great power, including its permanent seat at the UN Security Council, the status of a nuclear-armed state and the privileged relationship with Washington. These benefits have enabled successive governments to avoid facing up to the widening gap between the rhetoric and the reality. Britain's glorious role in the Second World War, especially in the version constructed by Churchill, is a great source of national pride but a poor basis for policymaking in the modern world.

Over the decades, British governments have shown the capacity to make pragmatic adjustments to the country's shrinking relative position in the world – the winding down of the Empire, the withdrawal from east of Suez and the long process of joining the European Common Market to take three examples. But in the process, a wide gap has developed between the reality of Britain's position in the world and the public perception of it. This is largely because successive governments, while carrying out these strategic retreats from exposed positions, have failed to be honest with the British people. They have preferred to stick with sound bites such as Douglas Hurd's famous phrase about Britain continuing to 'punch above her weight', with its comforting echoes of exceptionalism. I had my own experience of this when preparing the 2010 Strategic Defence and Security Review as National Security Adviser. I was told firmly by a senior minister that the overall message was to be 'no strategic shrinkage', even though the defence budget was massively overstretched and cuts were inevitable.

The changing dynamics of global power have consequences for every country which relies on a stable set of international rules.

The EU without the UK is a different organization, with the fault lines more clearly exposed between member states. There are deep differences on whether the EU should have a genuinely global foreign policy, or concentrate its energies on its neighbourhood and internal reforms. America's allies in Asia – Australia, New Zealand, Japan and South Korea – are also having to adjust to the new reality of a generation-long struggle between the US and China for dominance in Asia. No other country, however, faces the same scale of disruption to its settled national strategy as Britain. And it does so at a moment of profound national weakness.

———

When I started thinking about this book in 2017, my argument was that the world was becoming more dangerous and unpredictable as great power competition sharpened. I expected that Britain would face a greater upheaval than other Western countries because this changing geometry of power coincided with Britain's decision to ditch its forty-three-year partnership with the EU and plough its own furrow as an independent country. As I wrote, everything that happened seemed to make the choices for Britain more urgent and more difficult. The country floundered into a much more decisive break with the European Union than even the most ardent Leave campaigners advocated during the 2016 referendum campaign, with no real plan for its future role in the world. The competition between the US and China sharpened into a generational struggle for dominance, pulling US attention away from European security at a time when Russia was becoming ever more reckless in its efforts to destabilize Western democracies. Then the Covid-19 pandemic struck, weakening economies, prompting nationalist responses around the world and putting international cooperation under severe strain. It tested to the limit the competence of governments and the resilience of their crisis management capacities. In the case of Britain, the weaknesses it exposed were clear in two unforgiving statistics. The country suffered the highest number of excess deaths in the first wave of the pandemic of any European country except Spain,[4] and the largest fall in GDP of any major industrialized nation in 2020.[5] The Johnson government elected so decisively in December 2019 failed to rise to the challenge either of effective crisis management during the pandemic or of thinking strategically in the Brexit chaos about the country's long-term interests.

Britain needs to make some fundamental choices. They will have a decisive impact on the security and well-being of every citizen. They will also define what Britain stands for in the world, how others see us and how much influence we can hope to have. Since the post-war years, Britain's national strategy has been built on two pillars: influence on global affairs through a close partnership with the US, and a leading role in European affairs via involvement in the various schemes of European coordination and then integration. Both those pillars are crumbling. The US has moved away from global leadership. Outside the EU, Britain is less useful to the US and self-excluded from whatever direction European integration takes.

There is an urgent need for a new national strategy. It cannot simply be laid down in a government document. It needs to be widely debated and to win a broad measure of public support, because it will shape the country our children and grandchildren inherit. I hope that this book will contribute to, and even in a small way encourage, such a debate. I spent forty years representing British governments within the international system, and came to know well the strengths and weaknesses of the UN, NATO and the EU as they grappled with crises of all shapes and sizes. I have drawn on that experience in considering the choices involved in working out a new place for Britain in the world. The book is not addressed to specialists in international relations, but to readers who are concerned about the current state of international turmoil, and would like to know what the prospects are for restoring some degree of order, and the implications for Britain and other Western countries.

The book begins by exploring the intense period of US–UK cooperation that created the post-war system of international cooperation, the reasons it lasted so long and the damage done to it by the 2003 Iraq War. The second part explores the readiness of British governments to make the hard decisions which lie ahead. It highlights three vital areas where they will need to be much more effective: setting priorities among the many threats and risks; rediscovering the art of longer-term strategic thinking; and making the most of the country's diminished powers of influence. The third section looks in more detail at the crucial choices about Britain's international role: how to protect British interests in the growing confrontation between the US and China; whether to give priority to revitalizing institutions like the UN and NATO or cut a dash with an independent foreign policy and new alliances; how to balance Britain's need for trade and investment with standing up for human rights and democracy; and whether close defence and security links with European countries should take second place to a new emphasis on the Indo-Pacific region.

With events moving at a disorienting pace, I am aiming at a moving target with the conclusions in this book. But whatever surprises are in store in the coming years, the hard choices are already clear. The global response to Covid-19 has shown how quickly the habits of multilateral cooperation developed so patiently over seventy years can break down under intense pressure. One possible path for the future would be a return to nationalism, protectionism and spheres of great power influence. This book will make the case for a different approach. Britain's interest is to be at the heart of a new surge of international cooperation, matching the one which created the post-war institutions, and building on what has worked over the past seventy years. That would mean British governments giving priority to repairing the damage done in recent years to the country's reputation, restoring confidence in the UK as a creative problem-solver at the heart of the international system and rebuilding relationships with our European neighbours. All these will be essential if Britain is to promote its interests successfully in the world of tomorrow.

PART I

How We Got Here

1

IMAGINING THE POST-WAR ORDER

The Atlantic Charter, the United Nations and global security

The UN was not created to take mankind to heaven, but to save humanity from hell.
Dag Hammarskjöld, UN Secretary-General[1]

Breakfast in Placentia Bay

As a young member of the Foreign and Commonwealth Office (FCO), I would sometimes be sent on a nerve-wracking errand to deliver a file to the Permanent Under-Secretary (PUS), who occupied a vast and rather gloomy room in one corner of the building, immediately below the Foreign Secretary. I remember being intrigued by a document that hung on the wall of the PUS's office. It was a draft of the 1941 Atlantic Charter, with manuscript changes in Churchill's unmistakeable hand.

When, thirty years later, I became PUS and moved into the same office, I asked the FCO historians to dig up the document and put it back in the same place. I would often look at it and think of the extraordinary circumstances in which it was produced, the way in which it had shaped the landscape of my working life, and the central role my wartime predecessor, Sir Alexander Cadogan, played in its creation.

Cadogan is now a largely forgotten figure, but he had more impact on British policy during and after the war than many more famous names of the period. As PUS from 1938 to 1946, he kept a tight grip on the whole range of foreign policy and was the closest adviser to three Foreign Secretaries: Halifax, Eden and

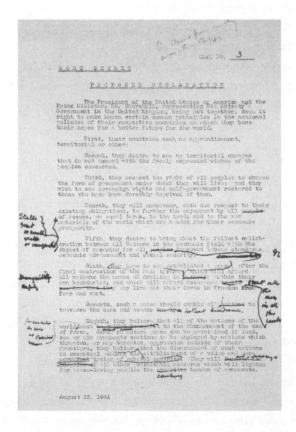

A draft of the 1941 Atlantic Charter with notes written in Churchill's unmistakeable hand. (© Foreign, Commonwealth and Development Office.)

Bevin. On top of that, he won Churchill's trust for his mastery of detail and shrewd judgement. Like his military counterpart, Chief of the Imperial General Staff, General (later Field Marshal) Sir Alan Brooke, he attended most meetings of the War Cabinet. These were often convened late in the evening and dragged on interminably as Churchill clashed with his ministers or advisers or both. Brooke would go in all guns blazing when he thought Churchill was wrong on military strategy, making no effort to conceal his fury and sometimes snapping pencils in his hands as a result.

Cadogan, although equally fearless in telling Churchill he was wrong on foreign policy when necessary, usually took a different tack – saying little, but making sure he was tasked with the follow-up. He would then labour deep into the night to come up with practical proposals to reconcile the differences around the Cabinet table. He had an uncanny ability to imitate Churchill's distinctive writing style, which he put to good use, for example ghost-writing messages to Roosevelt or Stalin in his master's voice. The next morning, he would take his work over to Churchill, who was often still in bed dictating to a secretary, cigar in hand, in the best of tempers, all the storm clouds of the previous night having cleared. The Prime Minister would sign off Cadogan's drafts often with barely a glance. With one more problem solved, the PUS would return with a sigh to a new stack of papers on his desk.

Churchill rated Cadogan so highly that he took him to all the great wartime summits, while Eden stayed at home to mind the shop. The first of these took place in Placentia Bay off Newfoundland in August 1941. There Cadogan showed his true colours – this super-competent and unflappable civil servant was also a man with a powerful vision of the future peace and a gritty determination to see it through into a reality in the post-war years.

After two years of war, Britain stood alone in Europe and was on the defensive in the Mediterranean. Japan was becoming increasingly aggressive in the Pacific. Churchill was desperate to get some commitment from Roosevelt about the circumstances in which the US would come into the war. So the British team prepared carefully, while HMS *Prince of Wales* spent four days and five nights zig-zagging across the Atlantic to avoid the attentions of German U-boats. One of their objectives for the summit was to persuade the Americans to issue a pair of parallel UK and US Declarations, with the American one warning Japan that any further encroachment in the Pacific would put them on a collision course with the US. In this Churchill was to be disappointed – Roosevelt was only willing to give the Japanese a vague warning accompanied by a suggestion of further talks. But at their first meeting on 9 August, Roosevelt sprung a surprise. He proposed a different, joint, declaration on principles for the post-war world, and invited the British side to draft it.

Churchill jumped at the chance. Cadogan recalled in a memoir written in 1962:

> Next morning (10 Aug), while I was having my breakfast on a writing table in the Admiral's cabin, I heard a great commotion and a good deal of shouting. It turned out to be the PM storming round the deck and calling for me. He ran me to ground and said he wanted immediately drafts of the 'parallel' and the 'joint' declarations. He gave me, in broad outline, the sort of shape the latter should take. I hadn't quite finished my eggs and bacon, but I pulled a sheet of notepaper out of the stationery rack before me and began to write.[2]

Permanent Under-Secretary for Foreign Affairs Sir Alexander Cadogan in his room at the Foreign Office in August 1941, the same month the Atlantic Charter was signed. (© National Portrait Gallery, London.)

Cadogan was the only expert on foreign affairs in Churchill's delegation, on a warship 2,000 miles from home, and without the time or the communications to get any help from London. In his usual unruffled way, he got to work and produced a text. As he put it:

> I had what I had written typed out and gave this first rough draft to the PM, who expressed general but not very enthusiastic approval. I think he made only one verbal change of no great importance. . .

Churchill passed on the text to Roosevelt. After several rounds of negotiation between Cadogan and his US opposite number, Sumner Welles, and then between Churchill and Roosevelt, the Atlantic Charter was agreed two days later (though the leaders never got round to signing it). The post-war order that would define the West for more than seventy years was initiated by this short document produced in such unpromising circumstances. It is all the more remarkable for being agreed between one country already in the thick of a fight for survival, and the other still a non-combatant nation with a strong isolationist lobby. It is worth looking at in a bit of detail because it laid the foundations for so many of the international structures which came to define the rest of the century.

Cadogan and Welles did not conjure up the Atlantic Charter from thin air. They wove together several strands of pre-war thinking. One source was President Woodrow Wilson's fourteen-point plan presented to the Versailles Peace Conference in 1919. This envisaged a 'general association of nations' providing 'mutual guarantees of political independence and territorial integrity to great and small states'[3] which became the basis for the League of Nations. The Covenant of the League committed members to a compulsory system of dispute resolution, including economic and, if necessary, military sanctions against a violator. It was an ambitious effort to prevent future wars. But the US Senate refused to take on a commitment that could have drawn the US into disputes anywhere in the world. Weakened by the absence of the US, the dispute resolution mechanism of the League failed during the 1930s in the face of Italian aggression in Abyssinia, and the Japanese invasion of Manchuria.

The League of Nations became a byword for an organization which had high ideals, but which was too weak and ineffectual to impose them. Wilson's idealism found another way forward when a group of US legal scholars persuaded French prime minister Aristide Briand in 1927 to propose a bilateral agreement with the US to outlaw war as an instrument of national policy. The US Secretary of State, Frank B. Kellogg, was at first reluctant, but agreed to pursue the idea in the form of a Treaty open to all nations. The Kellogg–Briand Pact (or the General Treaty for Renunciation of War as an Instrument of National Policy) was signed in 1928 by fifteen nations, including Germany and Japan. The parties agreed 'to renounce [war] as an instrument of policy in their relations with one another'. The Treaty declared new international law, but provided no mechanism to enforce it. For that reason it was readily adopted by the US Senate.[4]

The outlawing of war was one of the pre-war ideas that fed into the Atlantic Charter. Another was the importance of government action to promote the economic and social rights of individuals. This was very much a Roosevelt theme: it was part of the inspiration behind his New Deal programme in the 1930s in response to the Great Depression. Roosevelt repackaged this way of thinking as 'Four Freedoms' in his message to Congress in January 1941.[5] He took the opportunity to give his list a sweeping international reach:

> The first is freedom of speech and expression – everywhere in the world.
>
> The second is freedom of every person to worship God in his own way – everywhere in the world.
>
> The third is freedom from want – which, translated into world terms, means economic understandings which will

secure to every nation everywhere a healthy peacetime life for its inhabitants – everywhere in the world.

The fourth is freedom from fear – which, translated into international terms, means a worldwide reduction of armaments to such a point and in such a thorough fashion that no nation will be in a position to commit an act of physical aggression against any neighbor – anywhere in the world.

One Roosevelt adviser summarized the New Deal approach as 'the duty of government to use the combined resources of the nation to prevent distress and to promote the general welfare of all the people'.[6] Similar thinking was under way in the British government leading up to the Beveridge Report in 1942, which proposed a social security system and laid the foundations for the post-war welfare state and the NHS. The Atlantic Charter was, in some ways, the New Deal applied to international affairs.

The idea of a joint Anglo-American declaration of aims for the post-war world had been doing the rounds well before the meeting in Placentia Bay. Thinking in the State Department concentrated more on the economic than the geopolitical issues. One of the ambitions of the Secretary of State, Cordell Hull, and his Deputy, Sumner Welles, was to tie the British down to support for the principle of free trade, and therefore to abandon the system of 'imperial preference' which kept Britain's trade with its Empire shielded from wider competition. They also wanted to make sure the British would not enter into any secret treaties with other countries about frontier adjustments after the war, remembering how much these had complicated the settlement after the First World War.

When Cadogan sat down over his bacon and eggs to write out a first shot at this manifesto for the post-war world, he had this hinterland very much in mind – not least because he had spent several hours the previous day skirmishing with Welles on secret treaties and open trade. He was also Britain's foremost expert on the League of Nations, having been the UK's representative for a decade after 1923. Since the overriding British priority was to get the Americans as firmly committed as possible to the war effort and the international security arrangements that would be needed for an Allied victory, Cadogan took care that his draft gave great prominence to themes that would appeal to Roosevelt.

Cadogan organized his text into five principles. The first three survived virtually unchanged into the final version. The first and second principles followed the language of the League of Nations Covenant in committing both countries to 'seek no aggrandisement, territorial or other' and to oppose 'territorial changes that do not accord with the freely expressed wishes of the peoples concerned'. The third undertook that Britain and the US would 'respect the right of all peoples to choose the form of government under which they will live: they are only concerned to defend the rights of freedom of Speech and Thought without which such choice must be illusory.' The first phrase was Cadogan's way of reassuring the Americans that there were to be no secret treaties about frontiers in Europe. He and Churchill seem not to have anticipated the inevitable consequence that it was duly seized upon in India and across the Empire by all those campaigning for independence.[7] When he came to produce a revised draft, Welles changed the second phrase – he thought it would sound to US Congressional ears too much like an American commitment to enter the war. In his revised version, the third principle read less like a call to arms:

Third, they respect the right of all peoples to choose the
form of government under which they will live: and they
wish to see sovereign rights and self-government restored
to those who have been forcibly deprived of them.

Cadogan's fourth and fifth principles were the ones which proved
most contentious. The fourth covered the vexed issue of free trade
– or rather, in Cadogan's draft this was evaded. He proposed a
phrase so general as to be meaningless. The two countries would
'strive to bring about a fair and equitable distribution of essential
produce'. Having discussed the British draft with Roosevelt,
Welles made this point much blunter:

Fourth, they will endeavour to further the enjoyment
by all peoples of access without discrimination and on
equal terms to the markets and to the raw materials of the
world which are needed for their economic prosperity.

That in turn ran into the brick wall of Churchill's commitment
to imperial preference. He told Roosevelt over dinner on 10
August that he was determined to preserve Britain's pre-war
preferential arrangements: 'the trade that has made England great
shall continue, and under conditions prescribed by England's
Ministers. . . There can be no tampering with the Empire's
economic arrangements.'[8] When Churchill and Roosevelt
discussed the American counter-draft on the morning of 11
August, Churchill avoided locking horns with Roosevelt on
substance, and chose instead to play the timing card, asserting
that it would be very difficult to get quick agreement from the
dominions for a far-reaching change of this kind to the existing
trade arrangements. He was well aware that Roosevelt was

impatient to get the meeting finished and announce the results. Churchill's solution was a classic bureaucratic manoeuvre: to insert a get-out clause into the American text in the form of a qualifier 'with due regard for our present obligations'. To Sumner Welles's great disappointment, Roosevelt caved in and accepted.

The fifth principle in the final version of the declaration was an addition proposed by the British Cabinet. Churchill asked Clement Attlee in London as Acting Prime Minister to convene the Cabinet in the middle of the night, between the two main rounds of negotiation in Placentia Bay, to approve the draft he telegraphed to them. Attlee called the members of the Cabinet together at 2 a.m. – a remarkable feat, even in wartime. They made two suggestions, one on the trade article, which Churchill did not press, and another to insert a new article on social security:

> Fifth, they desire to bring about the fullest collaboration between all nations in the economic field with the object of securing for all improved labour standards, economic advancement and social security.

This boosting of the economic and social security content of the Atlantic Charter was a deft move by Attlee, as it played to Roosevelt's New Deal instincts as well as to British Labour Party policy. It was adopted without difficulty.

In the fifth and final principle in his original draft, Cadogan had lumped together three different issues – war aims, an international security apparatus for the post-war world, and freedom of navigation. In the course of negotiation, these were separated out into the sixth, seventh and eighth principles of the final document. The sixth, on war aims, could well have been difficult to agree, since the US was still not at war in August

1941.[9] But Roosevelt accepted a variant of Cadogan's formula. He incorporated references to freedom from fear and want but was also willing to accept the goal of an Allied victory, even though the US was still technically a non-belligerent:

> Sixth, after the final destruction of Nazi tyranny, they hope to see established a peace which will afford to all nations the means of dwelling in safety within their own boundaries, and which will afford assurance that all the men in all the lands may live out their lives in freedom from fear and want.

Cadogan's drafting on freedom of navigation became the seventh principle: 'Seventh, such a peace should enable all men to traverse the high seas and oceans without hindrance.'

The concluding eighth principle covered the vital question of the future international security machinery. Cadogan's formula of an 'effective international organisation' went too far for Roosevelt, who had not yet begun to prepare Congress for the prospect of the US joining any international mechanism. So he asked Sumner Welles to produce a counter-proposal which included the principle of outlawing the use of force (echoing the Kellogg–Briand Pact) and one of Roosevelt's favourite themes, the need for the complete disarmament of the nations 'which threaten or may threaten aggression outside their borders'.

That was as far as Roosevelt felt he could go without provoking his isolationists. But the ghost of the failed League of Nations was hovering in the room. Churchill pressed for something more specific on what the US and Britain were willing to do to implement the principles of their Charter. It was a crucial moment in the negotiation. He suggested that Roosevelt's language on disarming threatening nations should be followed by a declaration that this would be 'pending the establishment of a wider and more permanent system of general security'. Roosevelt, overriding objections from Welles, accepted this vague but pregnant formulation. The eighth principle is therefore a remarkable conflation of American idealism and British pragmatism. It embraces both Roosevelt's totally unrealistic dream that it would be possible to disarm all would-be aggressors, leaving the victorious Allies led by the US and Britain in the role of world policemen, and the successful British manoeuvre to get the US committed to the concept of a system of international security. It read as follows:

Eighth, they believe all of the nations of the world, for realistic as well as spiritual reasons, must come to the abandonment of the use of force. Since no future peace can be maintained if land sea or air armaments continue to be employed by nations which threaten, or may threaten, aggression outside of their frontiers, they believe, pending the establishment of a wider and permanent system of international security, that the disarmament of such nations is essential. They will likewise aid and encourage all other practicable measures which will lighten for peace-loving peoples the crushing burden of armaments.

This future system soon acquired a name. On New Year's Day 1942, after the US had suffered the Pearl Harbor attack and entered the war, Roosevelt invited Britain, the Soviet Union and China to sign a text based on the Atlantic Charter which was called a 'Declaration of the United Nations'. The following day, twenty-two other countries signed up.

When the British public learned about the dramatic circumstances of this first wartime summit held in conditions of such secrecy, there were high expectations that something momentous would be announced – perhaps a declaration of war by the US. Then they heard the terms of the Atlantic Charter read out on the radio in the matter-of-fact tones of Deputy Prime Minster Clement Attlee while Churchill was en route home. The immediate reaction was disappointment. Cadogan had been greatly buoyed up when Churchill (who was parsimonious with praise to his closest advisers) told him on the way home: 'Thank God I brought you with me!' But when he got home and heard Eden's downbeat assessment of the public reaction, he commented to his diary 'Gather Declaration was a flop'.[10]

The Atlantic Charter did little to help the Churchill government in the short term. But, over time, the principles Cadogan and Welles hammered out while sitting on a warship in the midst of a world war had a real impact. The ideas of territorial integrity and non-use of force went straight into the UN Charter which was signed in San Francisco in 1945, and thus became part of the backbone of international law on relations between states. The third principle became a rallying cry for the decolonization movement. The fourth pointed the way to the open trading system promoted by the 1947 General Agreement on Tariffs and Trade. The fifth endorsed the idea that economic and social security was a fundamental part of the responsibility of governments, championed in Britain in the 1942 Beveridge Report on the creation of a welfare state. And the historian of human rights Elizabeth Borgwardt traces the origins of the modern concept of human rights back to the sixth principle:

> . . .to speak explicitly of individuals rather than state interests – to use the phrase 'all the men in all the lands' in place of a more traditional reference to the prerogatives of nations – was positively revolutionary. The phrase hinted that an ordinary citizen might possibly have some direct relation with international law. . . though oblique, this hint that ideas about the dignity of the individual were an appropriate topic of international affairs was soon to catalyze groups around the world committed to fighting colonialism and racism as well as Nazism. It marked a defining, inaugural moment for what we now know as the modern doctrine of human rights.[11]

When I read this, I looked again at the draft of the Charter that had hung on my wall. It had one more surprise in store. I saw that the words 'all the men in all the lands' had been written into the text of the Charter at the very last moment in Churchill's characteristic hand. Among his many other achievements, Churchill can therefore be credited with being one of the founders – perhaps unintentionally – of the modern human rights movement.

Britain's hard-won reference to 'a wider and permanent system of general security' could have come to nothing. The US Congress could have refused to sign up to the UN as they had done to the League of Nations in the 1920s (despite President Wilson's passionate advocacy for the body he had done so much to create). In 1945, the US was in a position of extraordinary economic and military dominance, accounting for over 50 per cent of the world's GDP. American leaders did not need to bind themselves to a set of international rules. Indeed, all the precedents were against them joining. George Washington's 1796 warning in his farewell address to the US Congress – 'Tis our clear policy to steer clear of permanent alliances with any portion of the foreign world' – has rung in the ears of US statesmen ever since.[12] They traditionally avoided entanglements with the sorts of pacts and alliances which were familiar to European nations. However, in 1945, President Harry Truman and the Congress decided to accept the constraints of a set of international rules. They judged that this was the best way of encouraging the spread of democracy and open markets, enabling peace to spread and smaller countries to prosper.

Cadogan understood that it was not enough to plant the seed of the future UN in the Atlantic Charter. He and Anthony Eden were determined, once the Americans adopted the idea and began to draft what became the UN Charter, that Britain would put in the hard work to influence US thinking and, in the process, secure a prominent place for the UK at the heart of the post-war system. They bombarded Washington with papers on the future organization of the world, and inserted themselves into the drafting process more closely than any other country. It was Churchill and Cadogan who persuaded Roosevelt and Stalin at Yalta that France should be given the special status of a permanent member of the Security Council with the veto rights that came with it, although they got no gratitude from Charles de Gaulle for this massive and lasting boost to France's international status.

The London team also came up with creative solutions when the Americans hit problems. For example, they made a significant contribution on the issue of the veto rights of the permanent members. This was a central piece of the whole construction. The Charter gave the Security Council unprecedented legal powers to authorize the use of force, overriding the principles of national sovereignty and territorial integrity, in order to prevent or respond to acts of aggression. This in turn gave the Charter the teeth which the League of Nations had lacked. As a counterbalance, the veto right of permanent members was essential for both the US and Soviet Union. The US needed it to persuade the Senate to ratify the Charter. Stalin insisted on it to give him a free hand to use force if necessary in Eastern Europe (he soon found he needed it).

When the Americans unveiled their draft of the UN Charter to a wider range of countries at a conference at the Dumbarton Oaks estate in the Washington suburbs during 1944, it immediately became clear that those who were not to become permanent members hated the idea of the veto, which effectively divided the membership into first- and second-class status. The entire negotiation nearly collapsed over the issue. To break the stalemate, Cadogan and his team came up with an ingenious idea to sugar the pill for those who would be denied the veto. They proposed drawing a distinction between decisions of substance, for example on the use of force, where the veto would apply, and procedural matters, such as the Security Council deciding to hold a discussion, which would not be subject to a veto. The distinction was accepted by Stalin at Yalta. Other participants eventually accepted that it was as much as they were going to get, and the provision is enshrined in Article 27 of the Charter. It is still relevant to this day. For example, it allowed the Security Council to hold an open debate on the Russian annexation of Crimea in 2014, and so ensure a degree of accountability in the court of public opinion, even though the Russians could wield the veto to prevent the Council from adopting measures like sanctions.

The UN and international security

The veto power was essential to get the US and Soviet Union to sign up to the UN. But it meant that the Security Council was paralysed when the permanent members were at loggerheads. That was the case for much of the Cold War, which is why most of the high-level crisis management went on between Washington and Moscow. There was a brief golden era after the Berlin Wall fell in 1989, when President Mikhail Gorbachev's policy of cooperation with the West enabled the Security Council to act decisively after Iraq attacked Kuwait in 1990. It also made possible agreement on a large number of new UN peacekeeping operations, particularly in Africa.

But the shutters came down again with the divisions over Iraq and Libya and the growing resentment of a range of countries that the West had pushed the agenda of democracy and human rights too aggressively. The re-emergence of great power competition in recent years has pushed the Security Council once again into the background. That was painfully obvious in the case of the Syrian civil war. The patient mediation efforts of the UN Secretary-General's representative got nowhere against the backdrop of a divided Security Council. The major powers could not even reach a collective view when Bashar al-Assad used chemical weapons against his own people in 2013 and 2017. It was left to the US, UK and France to launch air strikes after the 2017 attack without a UN mandate.

Today, the Security Council faces a growing problem over its legitimacy because its membership has not changed to reflect the shifting geometry of global power. The difficulty of updating the membership as global power relationships evolve is a real flaw in its design. The UN General Assembly grew naturally as new countries became independent, rising from 51 founding member states in 1945 to 193 in 2018. It is a vast and unwieldy organization. But it can act as a sounding board and sometimes as a weather vane for shifts in global public opinion. This gives the UN Secretary-General a degree of moral force in speaking out on issues that concern the smaller countries who find it hard to get their voice heard.

The Security Council has only ever been expanded once, in 1965, when it increased from eleven to the current fifteen members. Reform efforts have dragged on for twenty years without getting anywhere. India, Germany, Brazil and Japan have campaigned as a group to be given permanent member seats, reflecting their economic weight. But any further expansion or a change in the status of existing members would require unanimity. There's the rub. Those with entrenched privileges will always have an incentive to block change. The US and Russia have not changed their position on the veto since 1945. France and Britain keep a low profile, paying lip service to the idea of increasing the membership of the Council, safe in the knowledge that the other permanent members could be relied on to take the flak for hanging on to their privileges. China as an emerging superpower wants both to keep its privileges and to refashion the international system to suit its purposes, while also enjoying its monopoly as the only Asian permanent member.

For now, China is pursuing two tracks: stepping up its influence inside the existing system and, in parallel, setting up new organizations, giving it new channels of influence. It works constantly in the Security Council to downplay human rights and civil liberties and to champion non-interference in the internal affairs of states. In an effort to present itself as a good global citizen, China stepped up its role in UN peacekeeping and took a more constructive line on reducing carbon emissions (all this has been undermined by its harsh crackdown on the Uighur community in Xinjiang and the democracy movement in Hong Kong). On the second track of establishing new institutions, China created the Asian Infrastructure Investment Bank in 2015 in a bid to rewrite the rules of the global economic system overseen by the Western-dominated International Monetary Fund and World Bank. The Obama administration saw this as a challenge to US dominance and was annoyed when the British government joined up. China also established the Shanghai Cooperation Organisation as a forum for economic cooperation in Asia. This did not get very far because China and Russia had very different visions of its purpose. So Chinese investment and political energy have gone instead into its Belt and Road initiative to create new maritime and rail links between Asia and Europe, and thereby strengthen Chinese economic dominance as well as securing control of some strategically useful ports.

At Davos in 2017, Xi Jinping set out the ambition for China to 'lead the reform of the global governance system with the concepts of fairness and justice'. An international system based on Chinese principles of fairness and justice would be very different to the one shaped by the Americans and British in the 1940s. But China's authoritarian system of control and surveillance holds attraction for many countries disillusioned with the liberal Western approach to human rights and social issues. The capacity of that system to impose draconian restrictions on the population was demonstrated in the pandemic.

The Security Council cannot manage fundamental differences of approach between the major powers. There is therefore no prospect of the UN playing a central role in international security for as long as leaders in Washington, Moscow and Beijing do not see it as in their interests to use this forum to settle their disputes.

But with national security increasingly focused on global threats to human health and the climate, the UN has a precious asset in its global membership and its network of specialized agencies. It has a vital role in fighting disease, poverty and malnutrition, in championing education and setting standards from employment rights to the governance of the internet. If properly organized and funded, it could also play more of a role in early warning of future hazards and planning for resilience in dealing with them.

What would Cadogan have made of how the UN has evolved from when he took his seat as the UK's first Permanent Representative to the new organization in 1946? He was above all a pragmatist, and would not, I think, have been surprised that the UN never developed into the sort of machinery for global governance that Roosevelt and Churchill, in their different ways, dreamed of. He would be frustrated that the necessary concession of the veto right for a select few has often left the Security Council incapable of using the formidable powers given it by the Charter. He would be disappointed by the inefficiencies of the sprawling bureaucracy that has grown up over the decades, but probably astonished and amused that the UN somehow manages to function at all with a membership of 193.

The UN today has many weaknesses. But it is the only forum with the power to make and enforce international law on relations between states, and the legitimacy that comes from its universal membership. The principles of the Charter offer at least some protection for medium-sized and smaller countries from the resurgence of great power nationalism. An organization with the range of the UN could only have been created in the immediate aftermath of a devastating event like a world war, which made radical choices possible. It would be impossible in today's polarized environment to reach agreement on any alternative global organization. The UN and its Agencies have an accumulated experience which no other international organization can rival, and the convening power to bring governments, business and interest groups of all kinds together in the kind of inclusive multilateralism that is the only way to tackle planet-sized risks to the climate, the digital world and public health.

Cadogan showed that, with a strong vision, hard work and creativity, it is possible to shape the international landscape. Britain's weight in the world is much reduced since the 1940s, and it cannot hope to have the same leading role in reforming the UN leviathan as it did in creating it. But it has a strong national interest in making the most of the powers of influence it still has to help adapt the global system to the new demands of the post-pandemic world.

2

MANAGING AN ALLIANCE
OF UNEQUALS

NATO and European security

*If we have to use force, it is because we are America;
we are the indispensable nation. We stand tall and
see further than other countries into the future.*
US Secretary of State Madeleine Albright, 1998[1]

European security in the Cold War

Those dining out in Vienna in the mid-1970s might have stumbled on one of the more bizarre rituals of the Cold War. Once a week, a group of ambassadors from NATO and Warsaw Pact countries took over the back room of a restaurant. As the evening wore on, a burly American handed round songbooks and called out numbers. The ambassadorial collective responded not with hymns, but with popular songs, alternately from East and West: British music hall classics, numbers from Broadway or Russian folk songs. The book featured songs from all the nineteen countries that participated in the Mutual and Balanced Force Reduction (MBFR) negotiations. The chorus-master for these occasions was the US Ambassador, Jock Dean. The British Ambassador, Sir Clive Rose, found that the sing-songs were far better than stilted diplomatic dinner parties at creating some camaraderie in a negotiation that would drag on for fifteen years:

> The Russian songs were in Russian script and phonetic Russian and in English translation. Songs like A Tavern in the Town, Swannee, Clementine, the sort of thing that everyone belts out. . . after dinner Dean would produce the song book which he would hand round and we would then sing alternately an Eastern song and a Western song. He would shout out number 25, number 43 and so on and it was a tremendous success.[2]

Journalists tried hard to get a copy of this East-West song book but never did. Clive Rose joked that it was the only NATO secret that never leaked.

The now largely forgotten MBFR talks conjure up what it was like to be an ally of the US during the Cold War. They were the only negotiations between NATO and the Warsaw Pact collectively. They showed that it was better to be in a voluntary alliance of democracies based on shared values, rather than an occupied country dragooned into the charade of the Warsaw Pact. The East Europeans toed the Party line in front of the Russians, but complained volubly to Western colleagues in the bars of Vienna that they were completely excluded from the policymaking.

The idea for the MBFR talks came from Nixon and Kissinger as part of their detente policy in the early 1970s. They were looking for a way to remove the Warsaw Pact's superiority in numbers of military personnel and equipment in Europe. They also wanted to derail a campaign by Senator Mike Mansfield to cut US troop numbers in Europe, by arguing that it would be better to hold off any cuts until this could be bargained against greater Soviet reductions. So they came up with a bloc-to-bloc negotiation to agree binding limits on the armed forces the two sides could maintain in a defined area of Europe. Kissinger also wanted a price he could charge Brezhnev in exchange for the Soviet demand for a Europe-wide security conference as a way of drawing a line under their invasion of Czechoslovakia in 1968.

MBFR therefore served a tactical purpose for the US and Soviet Union at a particular point in the Cold War. Yet what the negotiations were actually about was the long-term security and sovereignty of European countries. An MBFR Treaty would have put binding limits, for example, on the numbers of troops and tanks that a member state was allowed to have in an armoured regiment or fighter jets in a squadron. It would have constrained European members of NATO, all of whose armed forces would have been covered, far more than the US, which only had a small proportion of its forces in Europe.

This was the sort of encroachment on national sovereignty that led Charles de Gaulle to pull France out of the NATO military structure in 1966. France stood aloof from the MBFR talks for the same reason, while making sure they kept closely in touch with what was going on. I spent a lot of coffee breaks during my stint at NATO briefing my French counterpart on the (glacial) pace of the talks. All the other NATO allies apart from France not only accepted the prospect of binding limits on their armed forces, but more surprisingly that the bulk of the negotiating with the Soviet Union should be done by the Americans over their heads.

The US Ambassador, Jock Dean, and his Soviet counterpart dominated the talks to an extraordinary extent. The two of them met in the Hofburg Palace in Vienna (presumably ignoring the imperial connotations of that building) for weekly 'informal' sessions where most of the actual negotiating was done. Two other ambassadors from each side joined them on a rotating basis. But the American and Russian provided the continuity and did almost all the talking. And there was a lot of talking. Each week, Dean would sit down and dictate a supposedly verbatim account of the discussion, which often ran to 150 pages or more of typescript. On its arrival by courier at NATO HQ, this doorstep of paper was eagerly pored over by other NATO delegations for any sign of movement on either side.

The dominant role played by the US in European security through the Cold War was demonstrated again in the crisis triggered by the deployment of the SS-20 intermediate-range nuclear-armed missile by the Soviet Union in the late 1970s. This was a weapon which was widely believed in NATO at the time to have been designed for the political purpose of sowing division in transatlantic relations, since it had a range that enabled it to hit most of the territory of European NATO members but not the US or Canada. It thus played on the fear, never far below the surface in European capitals, of 'decoupling', that is, the risk that the US might not be willing to go to war for its European allies if the latter faced attack with weapons that did not directly threaten the US. As was typical in the Cold War, the Europeans looked to the US to find a solution. The Americans responded by leading a year of intensive work at NATO from which emerged what was known as the dual-track decision adopted in late 1979. The US would deploy, on the territory of its European allies, its own intermediate-range nuclear missiles that were capable of reaching the Soviet Union. Having shown Moscow that decoupling the US from its allies was not an option, the US would simultaneously offer to negotiate the removal of both sides' missiles.

Why NATO works

The UN and NATO are very different organizations, but together they formed the landscape in which Britain has pursued its security interests ever since. The UN was, as we have seen, global, with the vaulting ambition in the words of its Charter to 'save succeeding generations from the scourge of war'. NATO was a new kind of pact between like-minded countries. The 1970s arms control negotiations give an insight into how NATO operated at the height of the Cold War. This alliance of unequals turned out to be ideally suited to keeping Europe safe from the Soviet menace. But if it had just been a military pact against a specific enemy, it would have faded away when the Soviet Union collapsed.

The secret of its longevity is that it was and is both a collective defence agreement and a political alliance pledged to promote the values of democracy, human rights and the rule of law. The originality of NATO was that these two aspects reinforced each other. A member state could be confident that other members would come to its defence if attacked, not just because of words written in a Treaty, but because of the strength of the political commitment they shared to support the values of Western civilization. There had never been anything like this before. The dual nature of the NATO alliance was a stroke of genius. A lot of the credit for it goes to Ernest Bevin.

In the later stages of the war, Churchill and Roosevelt both believed that their partnership with Stalin – the Big Three – would continue to operate and that they would jointly oversee the subsequent peace settlement. Truman, who inherited the presidency on Roosevelt's death in April 1945, first met Stalin at Potsdam in July and immediately fell under his spell, noting in his diary: 'I can deal with Stalin. He is honest – but smart as hell.' As the Labour politician and writer Andrew Adonis brings out in his recent biography,[3] Bevin was clear about the threat Stalin posed to Western Europe from the moment he replaced Eden as Foreign Secretary, following the July 1945 general election. He too first met Stalin at Potsdam, but he had seen Russian communists at close quarters at international trade union meetings before the war. He understood the risk not just of a full-scale invasion of Western Europe, but also of Communist Parties coming to power (with help from Moscow) either through coups or through the ballot box. With the Communist vote running at 25 per cent in Italy and 20 per cent in France, this was a very real possibility. It took Churchill until March 1946 to recognize, in his Iron Curtain speech at Fulton, Missouri, the full scale of the Soviet menace.

Bevin focused initially on preventing a deal between Truman and Stalin, which could have led to the withdrawal of US forces from Europe within two years and a Soviet role in the administration of the whole of Germany. He pushed instead to get the British-occupied zone of Germany back on its feet economically as the core of a future sovereign West Germany. At the same time, he led the way towards closer political and security cooperation among the war-ravaged countries of Western Europe. He began with a UK–French security treaty signed at Dunkirk in 1947. Here, the focus was still on 'preventing Germany from becoming again a menace to peace'. Faced with such a threat, Britain and France undertook to give each other 'all the military and other support and assistance' in their power. A year later, Bevin brought together five countries – Belgium, France, Luxembourg, the Netherlands and UK – into an embryonic military and political pact: the Brussels Treaty on Western Union, signed in March 1948. By this time, most Western governments were coming to see Germany less as a military threat and more as an engine of Europe's recovery (although the French remained intensely worried about the risk of German rearmament). The Brussels Treaty therefore hedged its bets. It still contained a pledge that the signatories would 'take such steps as may be held to be necessary in the event of a renewal by Germany of a policy of aggression'. But the Treaty also called on the parties to consult together 'with regard to any situation which may constitute a threat to peace in whatever area that may arise'.

The threat they had in mind was increasingly obvious; the Soviet Union had organized a coup in Prague in February 1948 in order to install a Communist government. In response, the UK, US and France agreed to join their occupation zones in Germany in order to create an independent West German state, and to support it with Marshall fund money. In the summer of 1948, Stalin raised the stakes even higher with the blockade of West Berlin. Bevin set out his strategy for responding to the Soviet threat in a series of magisterial papers for the British Cabinet in January 1948. One was on the geopolitical challenge:

> If the Soviets secured control of France and French North Africa, of Italy and of Greece, and particularly if they could undermine our position in the Middle East, they would effectively dominate the Mediterranean and could (if they wished) deprive us of access to extensive markets and raw material, especially oil, without which our economic recovery would be difficult or impossible and the strategic position of ourselves and of the United States gravely jeopardised. . . If the USSR could gain control of China, France and a few other countries for international purposes, it would shift, politically, economically and strategically, the whole basis of power both in the United Nations and in the world at large.[4]

A separate paper considered what Britain should do about this threat:

> It is not enough to reinforce the physical barriers which still guard our Western civilisation. We must also organise and consolidate the ethical and spiritual forces inherent in this Western civilisation of which we are the chief protagonists. This in my view can only be done by creating some form of union in Western Europe, whether of a formal or informal character backed by the Americans and the dominions. . . We in Britain can no longer stand outside Europe and insist that our problems and positions are quite separate from those of our European neighbours.[5]

Even while he was working on bringing the Western European countries together in the Brussels Treaty, Bevin was also developing the idea of a transatlantic pact, incorporating a security guarantee but also a mission to defend the values of Western civilization. A week before signing the Brussels Treaty, Bevin sent George Marshall (Truman's Secretary of State) a paper with the first outline of an Atlantic Pact which would become NATO:

> I think that the most effective course would be to take very early steps before Norway goes under, to conclude under Article 51 of the Charter a regional Atlantic approaches pact of mutual assistance in which all the countries directly threatened by a Russian move to the Atlantic could participate, for example the United States, the United Kingdom, Canada, Eire, Iceland, Norway, Denmark, Portugal, France and Spain when it has a democratic regime.[6]

Minds were moving in the same direction in Washington. Arthur Vandenberg, the powerful Chairman of the Senate Foreign Relations Committee, had already begun discussions with the State Department on what would become the Vandenburg Resolution (adopted by the Senate in June 1948). This signalled that the Senate was open to the idea of US participation in collective defence pacts – something which had long been anathema in US foreign policy. Knowing of Vandenberg's initiative, Marshall was in a position to give Bevin an immediate positive response to his message in March: 'we are prepared to proceed at once in the joint discussions on the establishment of an Atlantic security system.'

NATO has proved to be remarkably durable and adaptable. The secret of its success is that the Treaty found an elusive point of balance between a strong political commitment to collective defence and maximum discretion for member states on how to implement it. This is captured in the tortuous wording of the famous Article 5, the hardest-fought lines in the Treaty:

> The Parties agree that an armed attack against one or more of them in Europe or North America shall be considered an armed attack against them all and consequently they agree that, if such an armed attack occurs, each of them, in exercise of the right of individual or collective self-defence recognised by Article 51 of the Charter of the United Nations, will assist the Party or Parties so attacked by taking forthwith, individually and in concert with the other Parties, such action as it deems necessary, including the use of armed force, to restore and maintain the security of the North Atlantic area.

It does not commit any party to the Treaty to any specific action, only to take 'such action as it deems necessary' (in order to satisfy the Senate), but also 'including the use of armed force' (to reassure the Europeans that the US would be at their side if really necessary). The political and moral obligation is strong, but there is no binding legal obligation or pooling of sovereignty involved. That gave NATO the flexibility to adapt as circumstances changed.

US accounts of the creation of NATO tend to focus on the tussle between the administration and Congress in finding that point of balance at the fulcrum of the Treaty.[7] Of course, NATO would not have happened if the Senate had not been willing to follow through on the Vandenberg Resolution and approve US participation in the new organization. But Bevin's role was also central. Having been a catalyst for the idea of a transatlantic security pact, he was also at the heart of the web of transatlantic exchanges as the draft treaty took shape. When in early 1949 the US administration went wobbly on the phrase 'including military force' under pressure from isolationist senators, it was Bevin who sounded the alarm. He sent Dean Acheson (who had just taken over from Marshall at the State Department) a stern warning on the impact in Britain and Europe of leaving out this phrase:

> The United States Government should not forget that our people will never be willing to risk once more being left to fight an aggressor alone and they will be deeply suspicious of any commitment which is based on the idea of the United States 'coming to the aid' of European countries as and when they see fit.

The phrase about military force went back into the Treaty.

Within months of NATO's creation, the Soviet Union caught Washington by surprise by detonating its first nuclear weapon. The deepening Cold War brought home to American policymakers how much they needed allies in Europe. The founding document of the policy of containment, NSC 68, adopted by President Truman's National Security Council (NSC) in April 1950, recognizes this:

> With the US in an isolated position, we would have to face the probability that the Soviet Union would quickly dominate most of Europe, probably without meeting armed resistance. . . this would in the end therefore condemn us to capitulate or to fight alone and on the defensive. . . In summary, we must, by means of a rapid and sustained build-up of the political, economic and military strength of the free world and by means of an affirmative program intended to wrest the initiative from the Soviet Union, confront it with convincing evidence of the determination and capability of the free world to frustrate the Kremlin design of a world dominated by its will.[8]

President Eisenhower's NSC adopted an even more explicit statement of the same US interest in document 162/2 of 1953, no doubt reflecting the experience of the Korean War:

> . . .the United States cannot, however, meet its defense needs, even at exorbitant cost, without the support of allies. . . The United States needs to have aligned on its side in the world struggle, in peace and in war, the armed forces and economic resources and materials of the major highly-industrialized non-communist states.[9]

49

NATO was the place where this balance of dependence between the US and its allies was managed. The whole construction depended on mutual trust. That is why throughout the Cold War, all NATO members were careful to keep disputes from reaching the point where the fundamental US commitment to collective defence might have been called into question. When the US publicly opposed the 1956 Suez operation, London and Paris abandoned it – resentfully, but immediately.[10] Other NATO countries steered clear of the Vietnam War but avoided this souring their relations with Washington. The way US administrations handled crises like the SS-20 missile deployments reinforced the confidence of their allies that the underlying bargain in the NATO Treaty was holding.

The framing of both the UN Charter and the NATO Treaty showed what could be achieved when Britain and America shared a vision and worked together to turn it into a durable institution. The message for modern British policymakers is that exercising real influence on the structures of international relations takes powerful ideas, but also following them through with relentless persuading and cajoling – and a willingness to give brutally frank advice to the country's closest allies when vital issues are at stake.

The failure of European defence integration

The fact that membership of NATO does not involve any transfer of sovereignty has been one of the secrets of its success. The Treaty itself is concise, with fourteen tersely worded Articles identifying principles and goals, not seeking to prescribe every detail, leaving wide discretion for member states to develop and adapt the organization. For example, the large NATO integrated military command and planning structure rests on one short sentence in Article 3 of the Treaty committing the parties to 'maintain and develop their individual and collective capacity to resist armed attack'. The post of NATO Secretary-General does not exist in the Treaty, unlike the North Atlantic Council which is made up of ambassadors as permanent representatives of their governments. When I was the UK Permanent Representative, I and my colleagues sometimes had to remind Secretaries-General of this fact when they showed signs of becoming too self-important!

NATO is an intergovernmental organization. European economic development followed a very different model: the pooling of national sovereignty over sectors of the economy in a supranational body. This was the approach first adopted by the six countries which created in 1951 the European Coal and Steel Community,[11] and then greatly expanded in the 1957 Treaty of Rome among the same countries, setting up the European Economic Community (EEC). With all the machinery of Commission, Court of Justice, Parliamentary Assembly and the rest, that Treaty runs to 248 Articles, four Annexes and many Protocols. And that was just the start. With each successive revision, the treaties got longer and more complex.

The team who conceived this approach of pooling sovereignty to drive economic integration – led by the French civil servant Jean Monnet and inspired by the foreign minister Robert Schuman – had a shot at applying the same technique to the organization of European defence. They sought to create a European Defence Community (EDC) on the same pattern as the EEC. This project suffered the same tendency to elephantiasis as the Rome Treaty was to do. By the time the EDC Treaty was signed in 1952, once again by the same six countries, it amounted to 132 Articles and twelve Protocols. It set up similar centralized machinery with a Commission,

Parliamentary Assembly, Court of Justice, and a Council of member states. To achieve a genuinely common European army, the Treaty provided for the 'complete fusion' of the armed forces of member states with exceptions only for those countries which had defence responsibilities for territories outside Europe (particularly France) and the temporary right to withdraw forces in case of civil disorder or international peacekeeping duties (but only with the agreement of the Commissioners). The Treaty even laid down how the European army would be organized. Nations would contribute units in a standard structure. Soldiers would wear a common uniform and although each would speak their own language, the board of Commissioners would work in French (no surprise there).

The Treaty required member states to hand over the sovereign control of all or most of their armed forces to a supranational body with only limited opportunities for member states to exercise influence. The contrast with the approach adopted in the NATO Treaty could not be sharper. It was not long before opposition to the EDC arose, particularly in France. Charles de Gaulle surfaced from the depths of retirement in 1953 to fire a broadside at the Treaty for surrendering French sovereignty. He foresaw the Treaty leading to an American military withdrawal from Europe and creating the prospect of an increasingly strong German army with French troops attached as auxiliaries. In the end, French parliamentarians voted down the Treaty inspired by Monnet and Schuman.

The EDC debacle was a humiliation for France and it left a durable mark. For forty years, European security and defence was the sole prerogative of NATO. Working at NATO in the 1970s, it struck me as very odd that the subject we were dealing with was European security, but there was no collective

European voice in the debate. Although the EEC and NATO were both based in Brussels, it was as if we were on two different planets. The two organizations did not overlap at any point. European defence ministers occasionally met for coffee in the margins of a NATO ministerial meeting, in a format known as the Eurogroup, set up by Denis Healey when he was Defence Secretary in the 1960s. Their limited discussions of cooperation between defence ministries took place under the suspicious eye of the US Delegation at NATO, who were determined to avoid being faced with a concerted European position.

The effort to apply the model of European economic integration to the very different world of defence failed. The security of the nation is at the heart of national sovereignty, intimately linked to a country's values and its vital security interests. The EDC experiment showed that even in the federalist mood of Western Europe in the 1950s, giving up sovereignty over defence was a bridge too far. This is a message that today's proponents of a European army would do well to ponder.

In Europe, economic integration and defence proceeded on different tracks until the end of the Cold War. But the fall of the Berlin Wall at the end of 1989 brought back to the top of the agenda both the issues that had dogged European security since the 1940s. First, managing an unequal alliance where US and European interests did not always coincide. Second, channelling the frustration in European capitals that integration had made them a global economic force but with no involvement in the hard power world of security and defence.

Living with the indispensable power

For all Bevin's efforts to design NATO as an organization which was about more than seeing off the Soviet threat, it could still have unravelled as the threat of aggression from the East receded. President George H. W. Bush, who entered the White House at the start of that period in 1989, was certainly alive to the risk. In his 1991 National Security strategy, he predicted that 'differences among allies are likely to become more evident as the traditional concern for security that first brought them together reduces in intensity.' That proved prescient, but the stresses and strains were manageable until the rupture of the Iraq War in 2003. In fact, the first major crisis of the post-Cold War world marked a high point of cooperation in the UN and NATO.

The international response to Saddam Hussein's unprovoked invasion of Kuwait in 1990 was a model of how collective security under the Security Council's authority was supposed to work. By invading a small country with powerful friends, Saddam Hussein united the UN membership against him, and created what Machiavelli called the opportunity of a good crisis. George W. Bush seized it. It was his finest hour. He built the case that stability in the Gulf region was of strategic importance to the US, and that getting the UN Security Council functioning again on the basis of US–Russia cooperation was of benefit to the US in creating the conditions for a more stable international order. These arguments had wide international resonance.

In Britain, there was much emphasis on the importance of avoiding the mistakes of the 1930s, when the major powers stood aside while small states were annexed. Public opinion on both sides of the Atlantic accepted that the use of force with a UN mandate by the broad international coalition, which George W. Bush assembled around a core of NATO members, was legitimate. He preserved that support by limiting the operation to its political objective of liberating Kuwait, and resisted the temptation to go all the way to Baghdad and depose Saddam Hussein.

The disintegration of Yugoslavia from 1991 onwards was a much more demanding test of the transatlantic bargain at the heart of NATO. European members of NATO worried that the inter-ethnic violence which spread across much of the Balkans in the 1990s raised the risk of massive refugee flows and of conflict spreading to neighbouring countries. The urban warfare inflicted a level of suffering on civilians unseen since the Second World War and jarred painfully with the new mood of optimism about the future of the European Union, which would find expression in the 1992 Maastricht Treaty. For European public opinion, ethnic cleansing was an affront to everything the EU stood for. Faced with public demands to act, Britain, France and other European countries took the risk of putting lightly armed troops into the UN Protection Force in Bosnia, which aimed to separate the parties and provide humanitarian assistance.

In Washington, President Bill Clinton took a totally different approach. There was widespread opposition to putting US forces into either Bosnia or Kosovo both in Congress and in terms of public opinion. Clinton was unambiguous in 1994: 'the war does not pose a direct threat to our security or warrant unilateral US involvement.'[12] After the bad experience of having eighteen US troops killed while on a UN peacekeeping mission in Somalia in 1993, the Americans were determined not to put their forces under UN command or deploy with anything other than overwhelming force. They preferred to influence events on the ground from outside, through air strikes and airdrops of humanitarian aid. In the case of Bosnia, the acute tensions between the US and its European allies dragged on for three years as the civil war worsened.

The US hesitations put the transatlantic alliance under huge strain, because they suggested that NATO solidarity did not apply to crises which happened beyond the territory of member states and were only seen as a direct threat by some of them. If Clinton had continued to keep the Bosnia crisis at arm's length, it would have undermined NATO, perhaps fatally. It would have shown that NATO was not relevant to the sort of threats that were much more likely to arise in the post-Cold War world. Eventually, Clinton did move, more in response to mounting public and political pressure at home – particularly in response to the atrocities being committed by the Bosnian Serbs at the siege of Sarajevo in 1995 – than as a result of the increasingly urgent pleas from his European allies.

Madeleine Albright, Clinton's Secretary of State, was talking about action in Iraq in 1998 when she called the US the indispensable nation. But the term applies equally well to the political and economic muscle the US brought to bear in breaking the deadlock in Bosnia. The combination of US-led air strikes against the Bosnian Serb forces, and the driving force of America's most effective diplomatic gun-slinger, Richard Holbrooke, brought Slobodan Milošević to the Dayton peace talks in 1995. As part of the settlement, the US agreed to contribute to a NATO-led ground force in a peacekeeping role. Clinton had made a hard choice to put American boots on the ground to keep the peace in a part of the world where the US did not have pressing security interests. By doing so, he restored confidence in the transatlantic alliance's relevance in the post-Cold War period. NATO took on for the first time in its history a military operation beyond the borders of its members. The fundamental bargain had held – just.

The pattern began to repeat itself when Milošević sent his militias into Kosovo in 1998 in response to violent attacks on ethnic Serbs in the province by the Kosovo Liberation Army.

Clinton had learned some lessons from the Bosnia experience. The US was much more closely involved from the start in diplomatic efforts to stop the ethnic cleansing. It was NATO which brokered an initial ceasefire in October 1998 and the US which provided the leader for a ceasefire monitoring mission organized by the Vienna-based Organization for Security and Co-operation in Europe (OSCE). This group of unarmed civilians dressed in white to emphasize their non-combat role was not at all what the US would normally regard as the role for US personnel. But Clinton was showing more solidarity this time with his NATO allies as they tried to end the violence without military force.

The effort was never likely to succeed. I was the Foreign Office Director dealing with the Kosovo crisis and had seen at first hand in the summer of 1998 the burned-out villages and forlorn groups of refugees fleeing the violence of Serbian armed groups. I recall vividly the anger of my boss, Foreign Secretary Robin Cook, when news broke one weekend in January 1999 that a massacre of forty-five Kosovar civilians had been discovered in the village of Račak. His instant conclusion that this could not be allowed to go on was shared by his colleagues Madeleine Albright in Washington and Hubert Védrine in Paris.

The three resolved to ratchet up the pressure on Milošević by organizing a Dayton-equivalent conference backed by the threat of a NATO air campaign if the Serbians failed to agree a withdrawal of their forces. The US, UK and France co-chaired a surreal two weeks of talks in the splendour of the Château de Rambouillet outside Paris. The Serb and Kosovar delegations remained poles apart (although they got on better in the bar over endless beers and cigarettes). In a last-ditch effort to break the deadlock, the US negotiator Christopher Hill and my French counterpart and I slipped away from the conference one evening and flew in a small US military aircraft to Belgrade for a midnight meeting with Milošević in his gloomy presidential palace. We had come to confront him with the stark choice of pulling his forces out of Kosovo or facing NATO bombardment. He was oddly detached, seemed not to grasp the gravity of the hour, and finished up talking wistfully (over the inevitable heavy meat dinner) of retiring to spend time with his grandchildren in Greece.[13]

Soon after that, the Rambouillet talks broke down and the US led a seventy-four-day NATO air bombardment of Serbia and Serbian units in Kosovo, in which German Luftwaffe Tornado jets participated in their first overseas combat role in the history of the Federal Republic of Germany. Eventually, Milošević did pull his troops out, and the US contributed heavily to a NATO ground force that deployed to stabilize Kosovo.

Twice in the 1990s the US was persuaded to put its shoulder to the wheel when the security interests of European allies were at stake. The unequal alliance held. Blair summed up his conclusions on a decade of Western military activism in a speech in Chicago in April 1999 as the Kosovo crisis was unfolding: 'The most pressing foreign policy problem of the 1990s has been to identify the circumstances in which we should get actively involved in other people's conflicts.'[14]

The speech set a series of tests for deciding on future interventions, but the implication was that some would be needed in the future. It also included an important point about globalization, which was part of Blair's approach to the whole issue of humanitarian intervention: 'Globalisation is not just economic, it is also a political and security phenomenon. . . We cannot turn our backs on conflicts and the violation of human rights within other countries if we want still to be secure.'

The 9/11 terrorist attacks, planned in the badlands of eastern Afghanistan and bringing devastation to New York and Washington, bore out Blair's thesis that, in an interconnected world, security threats could come from anywhere. In the aftermath of these attacks, it was the Americans who called for action, and their allies who showed solidarity with them. But in other ways, the early stages of the Afghanistan mission seemed to follow the paradigm of previous interventions. After a heavy US air bombardment, the al-Qaida terrorists retreated, and the Taliban regime duly collapsed. Recognizing that Islamist terrorism was a threat to all Western countries, Blair volunteered Britain to lead a small NATO operation in and around Kabul which began operations in early 2002 without significant casualties.

Intervening in other people's conflicts is now widely discredited, largely as a result of what happened in Iraq in 2003. But up to that point, the post-Cold War interventions had enjoyed a high level of public support. George H. W. Bush's handling of the Gulf War earned him the highest approval ratings ever recorded for a US president (89 per cent). In the UK, opinion polls rose to a remarkable 92 per cent as operations progressed.[15] The Yugoslav Wars were largely a response to public pressure in Europe for something to be done to stop the ethnic cleansing. None of these interventions aimed at, or achieved, regime change. None involved many Western casualties. The Afghanistan operation began on a wave of solidarity with the US around the world. All this seemed to suggest that the judicious application of Western military force could reverse acts of armed aggression, stop inter-ethnic violence and bring lawless states to heel, with very few fatalities among Western soldiers.

The Afghanistan mission stretched NATO solidarity to the limit as it expanded from a search and destroy mission against the al-Qaida terrorist camps into a countrywide operation of some 150,000 troops, from fifty-four countries, to shore up President Hamid Karzai's regime against the Taliban insurgents. Many NATO countries stayed in Afghanistan for ten years or more, taking severe casualties in the process. The continuing terrorist attacks in Europe in the years after 9/11 at least showed that the threat from al-Qaida was common to all allies. That gave a broad enough basis of common interest to sustain allied support for this operation, even as it took NATO much further away from its geographical and cultural area and into terrain that it was neither trained nor equipped to deal with. It was not easy to explain to European public opinion that (as German foreign minister Joschka Fischer put it) German security began at the Hindu Kush. As the years wore on without much progress in improving the security conditions or governance in Afghanistan, and the Western forces became the problem rather than the solution, even the most loyal allies began to sidle towards the exits. That included David Cameron, elected in 2010 on a mandate to end the UK's combat role. But the wind-down was (reasonably) orderly, and NATO continued to run programmes training and mentoring Afghan forces even when the fighting forces went home.

The Iraq War broke NATO solidarity. It marked the worst breach in an alliance which had stood together in the face of common threats for over half a century. The differences were partly patched up, but the effect on Western attitudes to using military force has been lasting. That is the subject of the next chapter. Before coming to it, there is one other impact of the sudden collapse of the Soviet threat to consider – the way it reignited interest in giving European countries their own capacity to use military force.

Disappointing great expectations: the EU and defence

With the end of the Cold War, a wave of optimism and energy surged through European capitals. The institutional result was the Maastricht Treaty on European Union of 1992. That weighty document was mainly focused on accelerating economic integration, but it also set a new goal for the organization: 'the implementation of a common foreign and security policy including the eventual framing of a common defence policy, which might in time lead to a common defence'.

As a member of the FCO's Security Policy Department, I was one of the negotiators who spent long hours hammering out this awkward compromise between two distinct camps. One group, led by the French, wanted to revive the old 1950s ambition of a European capability to conduct military operations independent of NATO. The other (smaller) camp, led by the UK, fought a rearguard action to avoid any reference in the Treaty to 'common defence', which we saw as a slippery slope, undermining the core function of NATO. But we were outnumbered, and in any case John Major, who took over from Prime Minister Margaret Thatcher in late 1990, was keen to be seen as more pragmatic on Europe than his predecessor. We therefore gave ground, and allowed a reference to *common defence* into the Treaty. We insisted that it was tucked away at the very end of the long and complex sentence quoted above, hoping that we had put the idea off to the Greek calends.

The UK team also came up with another blocking tactic which involved trying to breathe new life into the moribund Western European Union. The organization had lingered on since its moment of glory in 1955 when it served as a bridge to bring West Germany into NATO. But it had been losing out for decades to the much more dynamic European Union.

The WEU did however have one advantage from the London point of view: its Treaty committed the organization to working in close cooperation with NATO. And, even better as far as London was concerned, was a specific statement that it would not duplicate the military staffs of NATO and would rely on them for information and advice on military matters. We in London therefore prevailed on other WEU members to agree in parallel with the Maastricht Treaty a declaration which defined the WEU as 'the defence component of the European Union and as a means to strengthen the European pillar of the Atlantic alliance'. This convoluted wording was intended to outsource European defence activity to the WEU. But we knew that this was delaying the inevitable. It was only a matter of time before the advocates of European defence autonomy came back for more.

New thinking in Paris and London was made possible by the arrival of leaders who shared an ambition to make the EU more effective in the world. President Jacques Chirac came to power in France in 1995 with an unusual background for a Gaullist. He had lived in America and was fascinated by US power. He was deeply frustrated by the inability of Europe to act forcefully in Bosnia, and made a concerted effort to rebuild the bridges which de Gaulle had destroyed between France and the NATO military structure. Blair's election in 1997 gave Chirac a British counterpart who was the most pro-European prime minister since Edward Heath. Blair ardently wanted to put Britain back at the heart of Europe. He was as frustrated as Chirac that the European countries, for all their economic strength, could not stop humanitarian atrocities in the Balkans. His new Defence Secretary, George Robertson, was open to the idea of closer military cooperation with European partners and made this a part of his modernizing 1998 Strategic Defence Review.

Blair and Chirac were determined to create European options for dealing with a future Bosnia or Kosovo without having to go cap in hand to Washington. That provided the impetus for a new effort to lay to rest the ghost of the European Defence Community once and for all. I was part of a joint working group which set to work on the problem in early 1998. But we had not found a solution by the time of the annual Anglo-French summit in December, in the Brittany coastal resort of Saint-Malo. On a cold evening, while Chirac and Blair had dinner in a deserted holiday hotel, weary officials sat down with a blank sheet of paper. By 2.30 a.m. the next day, we had an agreed text, to everyone's surprise. The Saint-Malo declaration, which the two leaders signed off later that morning, was a genuine breakthrough. The British accepted that the EU should develop a real, usable military capability and the machinery to plan and command military operations. The French agreed that this should be done in a way which did not compete with NATO.

We were also careful to avoid the mistakes of the EDC. The Franco-British plan involved no transfers of sovereignty to the EU over defence matters and the text was explicit that it would be an intergovernmental approach. The idea was that when the EU decided a military force was needed, it would be assembled from voluntary contributions from member states, on the NATO model. The EU would avoid duplicating the large NATO operational planning machinery which existed at Supreme Headquarters Allied Powers Europe (SHAPE) outside Mons in Belgium. The trick would be to use European military officers already serving at SHAPE to plan operations for the EU. The French also accepted at Saint-Malo that the EU would only act 'where NATO as a whole is not engaged'. They would never have conceded the principle that NATO would have first right of refusal in dealing with any given crisis, but that was the implication.

The news that the two strongest military powers in Europe had reconciled their differences on European defence had an electric effect on other EU members. Within a year, new structures were in place in Brussels to showcase that the EU was moving into the defence area – the EU has always been good at structures. Soon generals and air marshals were walking the corridors of an organization that had been the preserve of economic gurus. An EU Military Committee supported by a Military Staff sprang up, with an intelligence cell (another first for an organization which had never had to handle secrets). At the Helsinki European summit in December 1999, member states committed to a grandiose Headline Goal to be ready by 2003 to put into the field a military force of 60,000. In other words, they were thinking of peacekeeping operations on the scale of the NATO presence in Bosnia and Kosovo. They pledged that this would be sustainable for a year, meaning that they would need to come up with at least 120,000 personnel in total to allow for six-monthly rotations.

These heady ambitions turned out to be wildly optimistic. If there had been an opportunity to deploy a smallish European military force somewhere in the European neighbourhood in the 2000–2001 period, I am sure that Chirac and Blair would have insisted on giving their brainchild its first outing. But it was not to be. After 9/11, Blair lost interest in European defence. He was totally absorbed by the new threat from global terrorism and his alliance with George W. Bush. By 2003, the EU was bitterly divided over Iraq and the whole context had changed. The planets had moved out of alignment.

3

RETHINKING THE USE OF FORCE

The Iraq effect, the West and war

*You can do a lot with diplomacy, but with diplomacy
backed up by force you can get a lot more done.*[1]
UN Secretary-General Kofi Annan, 1998

The long shadow of the Iraq War

I was feeling the effects of jet lag as I made my way into the
Foreign Office on Saturday, 15 February 2003. I had just come
off the overnight flight from New York and had to thread my way
through crowds gathering in Whitehall for a huge demonstration
against a war in Iraq. I felt as if I was living in three worlds
simultaneously. Firstly, there was the intensive diplomacy that
Foreign Secretary Jack Straw and I were immersed in seven days
a week to bring Saddam Hussein to cooperate with the weapons
inspectors. Even then, I still harboured some hope that if the
Security Council kept ratcheting up the pressure on Iraq, Saddam
would offer enough cooperation to avert a war. The second
was planet Whitehall, sucked into the increasing momentum
of military preparations. Thirdly, there was the world outside,
where everyone could sense that diplomacy was faltering and that
the likelihood of war was rising by the day. The million people

who assembled in London that day were part of a global protest movement which showed the deep divisions about the war before the first shot was fired.

The sequence of three Security Council meetings in the run-up to the Iraq War in February and March 2003 were the most dramatic international events I ever attended. The Council was the forum where the final arguments were played out on whether to use military force to disarm Iraq of its Weapons of Mass Destruction (WMD). It exposed in stark terms the widening chasm on the Western side as the US and Britain opted for military force while France and Germany opposed this with increasing vehemence.[2]

The first meeting was dominated by the US Secretary of State, Colin Powell. The White House had drafted him in to provide what they hoped would be the 'Adlai Stevenson moment' of the Iraq crisis, a reference to the UN ambassador who dramatically revealed proof that Russia was hiding missiles on the island of Cuba in 1962. Powell's mission was to unveil the US intelligence that would demonstrate Saddam Hussein was pursuing WMD programmes in defiance of Security Council resolutions and under the noses of the inspectors from the UN Monitoring, Verification and Inspection Commission (UNMOVIC).

Straw and I were at the Council meeting to support Powell in a task which we knew he did not welcome. In an atmosphere of high drama, he proceeded to give a seventy-five-minute speech complete with grainy satellite images of an alleged chemical weapons plant and clandestine missile launch pads. I remember being particularly struck by an artist's impression of a mobile biological weapons production facility, which looked rather like a small whisky distillery mounted on the back of a truck. Colin Powell's statement laid out a mass of circumstantial evidence but did not produce the smoking gun. He came to regret bitterly having lent his authority to this presentation, which he described as a great intelligence failure and a blot on his record.[3] As a man of the highest integrity, he believed, I am sure, in the case he was making. But in the pressure-cooker atmosphere of the Security Council, his arguments wilted and failed to convince the undecided.

The second meeting in the sequence, held on 14 February, was French foreign minister Dominique de Villepin's moment of triumph. He and the other foreign ministers listened at the start of the meeting to a presentation from Hans Blix, the head of UNMOVIC. This failed to back up the American case and suggested that there were signs of the Iraqis starting to cooperate with the inspectors. Villepin cleverly exploited this in making the case for more time for the UNMOVIC inspections. He finished his speech with a rousing peroration on the theme that France was an old country with long experience and a mission to stand up for international cooperation and the search for a better world.

It earned him private groans in the British delegation, but an unprecedented burst of loud applause in the normally hushed surroundings of the Security Council. This response was more eloquent than any speech in showing the way that world opinion was moving.

The third occasion, on 7 March, was Straw's. By that time, the drums of war were beating loudly (the invasion was to begin on 19 March). But the London team were still working flat out to get the elusive further Security Council resolution. The aim was that this would leave Saddam Hussein in no possible doubt of what awaited him if he continued to string along the UN inspectors – and might therefore have led him to cooperate enough to stop the countdown to war. Straw knew that he would have to make the speech of his life if he was to have any hope of reversing the tide of scepticism rising around us. He and I rewrote his speech in the cramped cabin of Concorde on the flight over, the day before what was likely to be the last chance to avert the impending war. During a sleepless night in a New York hotel room, Straw rewrote the speech again. The air crackled with tension as we walked into the Council chamber on the morning of 7 March. We were confronted, as expected, with Villepin and others pressing the case for more time. Straw discarded most of his text and extemporized an intervention which took on the points made by others. It was a debating speech in the House of Commons style – in sharp contrast with the scripted interventions typical in the Security Council. He dramatized the widening gap with France by addressing a surprised Villepin sitting across the horseshoe table as 'my friend Dominique'.

It was an effective parliamentary performance, and it earned Straw his own rather more muted round of applause. But it did not change minds or affect the outcome. There was no further resolution. A coalition led by the US therefore went ahead with the invasion and occupation of Iraq while the international community was deeply split, and without a generally accepted Security Council mandate.

In those weeks of tension and drama in 2003, the Security Council tested to destruction the various arguments on how to deal with Iraq's failure to comply with Security Council resolutions, and the risks that Iraq's WMD could somehow reach Islamist terrorists and thereby pose a clear and present danger to the security of Western countries. It provided a brutal but effective court of public opinion. George W. Bush and Blair would have done well to pause and think again about proceeding after the failure in the Security Council. But by then it was too late and the momentum towards war was too strong.[4]

The shadow cast by the Iraq War was apparent very quickly. In the run-up to the conflict, most polls in the UK showed a majority of the public were opposed, but that Blair's impassioned case for dealing with the threat from Iraqi WMD had made some impression. In answer to the straight question 'Do you approve or disapprove of military action?', an ICM poll in March 2003 showed 38 per cent in favour and 44 per cent against.[5] A more nuanced set of questions in an Ipsos MORI poll brought out some of the factors that were influencing opinion. Asked whether military action would be justified in the absence either of UN inspectors finding WMD or Security Council approval of military action, only 24 per cent supported action and 63 per cent were against. If the Security Council approved, the support increased to 46 per cent in favour, with 41 per cent against. If in addition the inspectors found WMD, then 74 per cent favoured military action, with only 17 per cent opposed.[6]

When the efforts of Britain and others to get Security Council approval fell apart, and the invading forces failed to find the WMD which intelligence reports said were there, it was no surprise that public support dropped further and never recovered. By 2007, all polls in the UK showed support for the Iraq War below 30 per cent. A total of 179 members of the British armed forces died in Iraq. Many more were seriously injured. Hundreds of thousands of civilians in the Middle East have died in the years of insurgency that followed the Western interventions.

The cost in British lives was graven on the popular memory by the number of times the town of Royal Wootton Bassett, next to RAF Lyneham in Wiltshire, had to arrange a civic ceremony to pay tribute as the coffins of armed forces personnel who had died arrived back on home soil.[7] But military casualties are not the only factor influencing public opinion on any given conflict. Polls in the US and Britain have shown that people also take into account whether the military action has improved their security and the lives of people in the country conquered. One academic study of public attitudes in the US to the use of military force since 1945 concluded that 'the public is defeat phobic, not casualty phobic.'[8] Looking back in 2013, 70 per cent of respondents told an Ipsos MORI poll that Britain had been wrong to get involved. Only 12 per cent of respondents thought that the war had made the world a safer place. The three top reasons they gave for Britain's involvement being wrong were that the war had not served Britain's interests, that Blair had lied about WMD and that it had been a waste of the lives of British troops.

The Iraq effect is apparent in the automatic response of British politicians of all parties to any proposed use of military force – *no boots on the ground*. In discussing the approach to the military action in Libya in early 2011, Cameron says in his memoirs: 'One thing on which we were all agreed however was that the situation didn't warrant "boots on the ground" – a level of intervention that would never get past parliament.'[9]

Obama, reflecting on his own decision to take a role in the Libya operation which one administration official anonymously described as 'leading from behind',[10] was also clear that a ground-force deployment was never on the cards:

> So what I said at that point was, we should act as part of an international coalition. But because this is not at the core of our interests, we need to get a UN mandate; we need Europeans and Gulf countries to

be actively involved in the coalition; we will apply
the military capabilities that are unique to us, but we
expect others to carry their weight. And we worked
with our defense teams to ensure that we could execute
a strategy without putting boots on the ground and
without a long-term military commitment in Libya.[11]

In the Libya case, there was a good military argument that
introducing Western ground troops into the confused situation
of a developing Libyan civil war, with all its tribal cross-currents,
would rapidly turn them into targets. But the option was ruled
out on political grounds even before its potential military value
had been considered. That decision had consequences. When
the Gaddafi regime collapsed, the institutions of state had
been so hollowed out during his forty years of bizarre personal
rule that there was no authority capable of holding the ring
and preventing the descent into chaos. There was neither
the opportunity nor the political will on the Western side to
attempt to impose a Dayton-style peace settlement enforced
by NATO military forces. The plans coordinated by the UN
– with Britain's Development Secretary, Andrew Mitchell,
playing a prominent role – to get humanitarian assistance and
capacity-building support to the interim administration as soon
as the fighting stopped could not be implemented. The security
situation never allowed it.

The spectre of Iraq also haunted the discussions among the
Western allies over how to respond to the worsening violence
in Syria after mass protests broke out in March 2011. Cameron
recalls that he was determined that Britain should be in the
vanguard of supporting rebel forces but . . .

Supporting the opposition never meant Western boots on the ground in significant numbers. An Iraq-style military invasion was politically unsellable at home and abroad, and wouldn't have been right in this conflict anyway. But I knew that for the opposition to have any chance against the regime we had to go beyond this 'non-lethal assistance'. They would need our 'lethal assistance' – weapons, training and back-up from the air.[12]

Cameron spells out his frustration at trying to get a risk-averse British national security establishment to give him more adventurous options, and to 'get the generals out of their Iraq and Afghanistan mindset towards a more indirect approach based on training, equipping and mentoring irregular Syrian forces'.

His greatest frustration was with Obama, who, from the start of the Syria crisis, resisted pressure from his more interventionist advisers like Samantha Power, his UN ambassador, for the US to take a direct hand to avert a humanitarian disaster. After much agonizing, Obama agreed to a programme to train, equip and mentor the rebel forces. But he was determined to avoid what he saw as a slippery slope towards an Iraq-style intervention: 'The notion that we could have – in a clean way that didn't commit US military forces – changed the equation on the ground: that was never true.'[13]

The spectre of Iraq again loomed over the British House of Commons in August 2013, when MPs debated the use of military force in response to the harrowing evidence that the Assad regime had used chemical weapons against its own civilians. In many ways, the case was very different from Iraq in 2003. No one was suggesting dispatching ground forces into Syria. The proposal was not an invasion and occupation but a limited air strike to 'deter and degrade the future use of chemical weapons' by targeting 'the command and control of the use of chemical weapons and the people and buildings involved', as Cameron put it in opening the debate.[14]

Nonetheless, there were enough parallels to unsettle many parliamentarians. The government's contention that it was Assad's forces who used the chemical weapons rested partly on intelligence. Just before the debate, the government released a letter from the Chairman of the Joint Intelligence Committee setting out the key judgements from the Committee's assessment of the evidence. For understandable reasons, they could not release all the underpinning intelligence. But after their experience over Iraq, some Members of Parliament were suspicious that once again the government were exaggerating the strength of the intelligence. There were other parallels too. As in Iraq, there were UN inspectors on the ground who were due to report to the Security Council. Efforts were under way to get a mandate from the Security Council authorizing the use of force but, once again, the Council was split and the Russians and Chinese were blocking. Sensing the risk of defeat, the government conceded one of the Labour opposition's demands – that there should be a second parliamentary vote on military action after UN inspectors had reported and the Security Council had considered a resolution – just before the debate. For all those who had sat through the Commons debates on Iraq a decade before, there was a strong sense of déjà vu.

Cameron took the issue of Iraq head-on in his opening speech to a packed Commons Chamber, recognizing that

> the well of public opinion was well and truly poisoned
> by the Iraq episode and we need to understand the
> public scepticism. . . We must recognise the scepticism

and concern that many people in the country will have
after Iraq, by explaining carefully and consistently all
the ways in which this situation and the actions that we
take are so very different.

He was aware of the danger of appearing to base his case for
action on intelligence material that the House of Commons had
not seen, so he was at pains to emphasize:

I am not standing here and saying that there is some
piece or pieces of intelligence that I have seen, or the
JIC has seen, that the world will not see, that convinces
me that I am right and anyone who disagrees with me
is wrong. I am saying that this is a judgement. . .

Despite all these precautions, the tone of the debate was sceptical
from the start. Straw, who knew better than anyone how
damaging the exaggeration of the intelligence case over Iraq had
been, commented that the government had yet to prove their case
that the chemical weapons had definitely been used by the Assad
regime. He noted acidly that 'there was also very strong evidence
about what we all thought Saddam held' by way of WMD. He
went on to make the crucial point that 'one of the consequences
of the intelligence failure on Iraq has been to raise the bar that
we have to get over when the question of military action arises.'
Other backbenchers chimed in. Many Labour MPs questioned
whether the government had yet produced compelling evidence
of Assad's responsibility; they were wary of relying on intelligence
judgements – as one put it, 'those of us who were here in 2003 at
the time of the Iraq War felt they had their fingers burnt.' They
therefore wanted to pause long enough to see the UN inspectors'

report, and to give time for a real effort to get a Security Council mandate. Some were worried about what a one-off air strike would achieve, whether it would suck Britain into another Middle East war, and why it had to be Britain again taking action.

In summing up the government's case at the end of the debate, Deputy Prime Minister Nick Clegg tried to reassure all the doubters that 'this is not an attempt to barge our way into someone else's war. . . We are not talking about putting boots on the ground.' The doubters were not convinced and the government lost the vote by a narrow margin of 272 in favour and 285 against. It was the first time the British government had lost a vote on the use of military force since 1782, when Parliament insisted that the war against the colonies in America should end.

It turned out that the leader of those former colonies had his own doubts about military action in 2013. Obama had laid down a clear red line that the US would not tolerate the use of chemical weapons by the Assad regime. But after Cameron's defeat in the House of Commons, Obama did a U-turn and put the issue of a US military strike to the Congress, wrong-footing his administration in the process and effectively ensuring that there would be no US military response. Reflecting later, he saw this as a defining moment of his international policy, the moment he broke free from what he saw as the Washington policy establishment's tendency to turn automatically to military options:

Where am I controversial? When it comes to the use of military power. . . That is the source of the controversy. There's a playbook in Washington that presidents are supposed to follow. It's a playbook that comes out of the foreign-policy establishment. And the playbook prescribes responses to different events, and these responses tend to be militarized responses. Where America is directly threatened, the playbook works. But the playbook can also be a trap that can lead to bad decisions. In the midst of an international challenge like Syria, you get judged harshly if you don't follow the playbook, even if there are good reasons why it does not apply.[15]

Contrasting strengths: NATO, the EU and the use of force

Obama's approach of leading from behind in Libya was the first clear evidence that US security priorities had shifted as a result of the Iraq War. The Europeans could no longer count on the Americans to join in their expeditionary wars. But the position Obama took on this issue was still compatible with a firm US commitment to come to the defence of a NATO ally if they were attacked. Trump openly questioned the value of NATO during the 2016 election campaign and throughout his time as president. This was much more corrosive of the fundamental NATO bargain, especially when he coupled it with the suggestion that he would only come to the defence of countries that were meeting the goal endorsed by all NATO members at a summit in Wales in 2014 that they would aim to spend 2 per cent of gross domestic product on defence.

Many European countries were spending well below that for most of the period after 1989. They were far quicker than the US to take the peace dividend – while expecting the US protective umbrella to remain in place. By 2018, US defence spending amounted to 71 per cent of NATO's combined defence expenditure, while the US economy was only 51 per cent of the combined GDP. With justification, successive US presidents complained that the Europeans and Canadians were free-riding on the massive US defence budget. Germany, for example, cut its defence spending to 1.1 per cent. Trump's much rougher approach to NATO allies may have had some impact. But the decisive influence was the 2014 Russian invasion of Ukraine. Defence spending among non-US NATO members began to rise from that time. The NATO Secretary-General confirmed in late 2020 that, over the years since 2014, defence spending in the NATO members apart from the US had grown from $250 billion to $313 billion a year. Ten member states met the 2 per cent target, up from three in 2014. Germany increased its defence spending by 40 per cent in the period, with defence as a share of GDP rising from 1.2 per cent to almost 1.6 per cent.[16] France announced a sharp increase in defence spending in 2018, and Britain did the same in 2020 despite the economic pressures of the pandemic.

This takes the spending of both countries well above the NATO target, in Britain's case to 2.2 per cent.[17] All this extra spending will take time to translate into military capabilities. But NATO is already better prepared militarily for its core task of territorial defence than at any time since the Cold War. The US, Britain and other NATO members deployed combat-ready forces to Poland and the Baltic States from 2016. The Pentagon spent $2.2 billion on pre-positioning warfighting equipment in Europe. President Biden understands the value of allies to the US. With his arrival, the doubts in other NATO capitals as to whether the US still stands behind the core bargain of mutual solidarity rapidly fell away. But the Biden administration will expect its allies to sustain the increase in defence spending. And NATO still faces searching questions on whether its members share a strategic purpose around which all can rally.

_____

The EU has also struggled to agree about its role in the world, and especially its attitude to military power. The momentum towards a European military capability generated between the British and French with their 1998 Saint-Malo initiative was not entirely snuffed out by the Iraq War. But it was dramatically slowed. The EU took over the 7,000-strong peacekeeping mission in Bosnia from NATO in 2004.[18] But that was the biggest military operation it ever conducted. The EU soon dropped any idea of duplicating large-scale military peacekeeping operations, recognizing implicitly that NATO was much better adapted for this role. Instead, the EU developed a 'comprehensive approach' to promoting its interests and values by combining economic muscle with political influence, the benefits of its large development budget, and where necessary relatively small commitments of military forces in training or monitoring roles. A recent academic study[19] of the twelve purely military missions undertaken by the EU found that overall the organization 'remains a rather risk-adverse military actor that is quite selective in the military missions it engages in and has a strong preference for missions with relatively low levels of military robustness'.

Since 2007, the EU has nominally had two battlegroups (battalion-sized units of around 1,500 personnel) at high readiness to deploy on peacekeeping or humanitarian missions. But they have never been used. Twenty years after the Saint-Malo breakthrough, the EU had 5,000 personnel deployed in ten civilian missions and six military missions.

The EU's ambitions on defence have often been mocked in Britain, with suggestions that they could lead to a European army commanded by the President of the European Commission. That is patent nonsense. From Saint-Malo onwards, all the texts on European defence have been clear that cooperation in this area, as with foreign policy, lies in the intergovernmental part of the EU Treaty structure. Indeed Article 4(2) of the Treaty is explicit that 'national security remains the sole responsibility of each member state.' The EDC put a stake through the heart of the idea of a European army under supranational control. But the question remains whether the EU in its intergovernmental guise, symbolized by the heads of state and government sitting around the table in the European Council, could ever in practice replace NATO in conducting a warfighting mission.

Everything about the EU makes it the wrong choice for such a role. The EU's culture and organization stem from its roots in regulating economic integration. The various EU institutions – the Commission, the European Court of Justice, the European Parliament and the Council – all have their treaty-based roles and statutory rights. The whole structure is built on the French administrative law tradition, which means careful attention at every stage to precedent and legal base. The style is deliberative. Information is widely shared and the checks and balances mean that tempo is often leisurely. Military operations, with their need for rapid decision-making on unexpected issues and with conflicting information, are the polar opposite of what the EU is optimized for. By contrast, NATO was designed as an organization to plan and command military operations. It has built up seventy years of experience in setting standards of operability among the armed forces of member states and a well-tried military command chain. This was helped by its shape as an unequal alliance with one dominant member providing by far the largest share of military resources – and the Supreme Commander.

The most striking illustration that the EU is not the right organization to oversee serious combat operations is that the most ardent advocate of European autonomy – France – in practice chooses not to use the EU for conducting its military operations. French armed forces have taken part in NATO operations in the Balkans and Afghanistan, and in US-led coalitions such as the air campaign against ISIS in Syria. They have run military operations on a national basis, as in the case of Mali, and jointly with Britain, in the Libya air campaign. But they have never proposed an EU combat operation.

There are two further developments which have raised the bar on any possible use of force even higher for Western democracies: sustaining public support in the maelstrom of instant communications and coping with the growing role of judges in scrutinizing what happens on the battlefield. Neither ties the hands of authoritarian rulers to anything like the same extent.

War in the digital age

The Iraq experience left politicians and the public on both sides of the Atlantic feeling they had been misled into a war which turned out to damage both regional security and Western interests. The conclusion was clear: that this should never happen again. In addition, the political risks, in a democracy, of resorting to the use of force were rising in the era of instant communications.

The problem of keeping public support for military operations in the face of graphic press reports from the battlefield is not new. It has confronted governments since war correspondents first got access to the wireless telegraph in the middle of the nineteenth century. Television was already a major factor by the time of the Vietnam War. But the arrival of instant digital communication from anywhere on the planet has increased the saturation of media – and now social media – coverage to the point where the information war is a decisive part of any military campaign.

During the 2011 Libya bombing campaign, the quickest way for decision-makers in London to know what was happening was not to ask the Chief of Defence Staff, but to watch Sam Kiley reporting for Sky News in real time from the Libyan side of the front line. No military communications system could match that for speed. The maelstrom of digital information has far-reaching consequences for the conduct of military operations. There is no longer any real distinction between the strategic level inhabited by politicians and senior commanders, and the tactical level where the fighting is done. Graphic images of death and destruction available on every smartphone can rapidly undermine public support for military action, however worthy the objective. Political leaders have to react very fast, for example to allegations about civilian casualties or mistreatment of detainees by Western troops. And the openness of Western societies gives adversaries every opportunity to shape opinion with fake news and fabricated atrocities.

The scope to manipulate public opinion by flooding social media with disinformation has the potential to wreck public support for a military operation however strong the case for it may be. It reinforces all the other pressures on politicians to show that they are in charge. Once they cross the Rubicon by using armed force against an adversary, previously cautious ministers rapidly become impatient for results and willing to take risks to get them, as pressures mount to show that their gamble is paying off. David Cameron comments in his memoirs:

People assume the job of Prime Minister is simply to take
the big decision, issue the decree, as it were, and then
consider it done. But the Libya campaign brought home
to me that so much of the job isn't just the deciding –
it's the doing: cajoling, corralling, convening meetings,
questioning official advice, offering up new solutions,
being creative, seeking wider opinions, and keeping on
and on at people until something happens.[20]

The transparency created by digital media means almost instant
accountability to press and parliaments for everything that
happens in a military campaign (and the things that don't happen
but which are inserted into the public debate by disinformation
and manipulation). Political leaders are therefore driven to
demand a degree of hands-on involvement which feels to their
military commanders like micromanagement. Again, there is
nothing new in this phenomenon. Churchill appointed himself
Minister of Defence and held on to that position throughout the
Second World War, precisely in order to give himself that power.

Other renowned war leaders like Clemenceau and Lincoln
were also notorious for interfering constantly with their
military commanders.[21] Now, modern technology makes
micromanagement alarmingly easy. The pictures of Obama
and his national security team watching the dramatic assault by
helicopter-borne US Navy SEALs on Osama bin Laden's hideout
in Pakistan in 2011 spoke volumes. Imagine if Churchill had
been able to look over the shoulders of his commanders and
interfere with their decisions in real time.

The current generation of political leaders is the first to have
both the insatiable demand for instant reaction generated by
social media and the technology that enables them to meddle

from thousands of miles away, inserting what the military call the 2,000-mile screwdriver. These pressures will only get worse as the digital revolution continues to sweep away the old barriers of time and distance. And they apply disproportionately in democratic countries. Western politicians are subject to public and parliamentary pressures that authoritarian leaders habitually suppress. Democratically elected politicians cannot censor the internet or stifle criticism in the press. They cannot evade accountability. The commitment of democratic countries to openness and the rule of law is a huge strength, which differentiates them from authoritarian regimes. But it gives adversaries opportunities to undermine public support and cohesion using the tools of our open society. These weapons could be particularly effective in sowing doubt and discord during a military conflict, when public anxieties in Western countries would already be acute, and support for the risks of military action brittle.

The fog of law

One other Iraq effect applies specifically to European countries, with a particular impact in Britain. That is the encroachment of human rights law into the conduct of military operations. Military personnel have not been, and should never be, above the law. But their profession involves combat, and therefore killing people. A specific body of law, international humanitarian law, has grown up over the last 150 years, codified in the Geneva Conventions. They were drafted to apply to wars between states and, in particular, to protect civilians caught up in such wars. Human rights law was first set out in the European Convention on Human Rights (ECHR). This was adopted in 1950 by another of the great post-war institutions, the Council of Europe, a grouping of governments and parliaments founded in 1948 and taking its inspiration from Churchill.[22] The ECHR protects a range of crucial individual rights, including the rights to life, to liberty and security, to a fair trial and to free expression. It prohibits torture and inhuman and degrading treatment, and created the European Court of Human Rights at Strasbourg to exercise jurisdiction over this new body of international law.[23] The Convention was designed to apply in peacetime, and gave parties the right to derogate under Article 15 in situations of 'war or other public emergency threatening the life of the nation'.

The British and other European governments did not ask for any derogation from the ECHR during their military operations in the Balkans, Iraq or Afghanistan, since they did not consider that the Convention applied outside the territories of the signatory states. However, the judges of the Strasbourg Court thought otherwise. They concluded that the Convention applied to the armed forces of signatory states when they were engaged in military operations and holding territory in another country.[24] The first move in this direction was a judgment in 2011[25] that, in the absence of any derogation from the Convention, Iraqi nationals were entitled to its protection when British occupying forces were responsible for security in the Basra area from 2003. This case opened the way for European (and British) human rights law to follow British troops onto the battlefield abroad. Later judgments by British courts,[26] following the logic of the European court ruling, found that the right to life in Article 2 of the ECHR applied to UK soldiers in Iraq, and made it possible for the families of any British soldier killed or injured in combat to bring civil cases against the British government for negligence.

The Strasbourg Court judgments extending the ECHR's protection of the right to life to soldiers in combat potentially put military commanders in an impossible situation. These judgments were hard to reconcile with the Geneva Conventions, which recognized, for example, that it was the duty of soldiers in wartime to kill the enemy and to risk being killed. As Professor Charles Garraway of the University of Essex observed in giving evidence to the House of Commons Defence Select Committee: 'Those who argue that the law of armed conflict is subservient to human rights law in all circumstances are effectively declaring that it is impossible for the UK armed forces to conduct high intensity operations.'[27]

A military commander could as a result be subject to two competing legal standards, for example when faced with the highly sensitive issue of the detention of suspects. During the Iraq War, the occupying forces (including Britain) were authorized by UN Security Council Resolutions to intern suspects. Their treatment was already regulated by Geneva Protocol IV on Civilian Internment in the Interests of Security. Despite this, the Strasbourg Court found in the case of one Iraqi citizen detained by British forces that his rights under Article 5 of the ECHR on liberty and security had been breached.[28]

A detailed review of the judgments by the British and Strasbourg courts applying human rights law concluded that they had created a 'Fog of Law', and that 'it is clear that there are now very good reasons to fear that many actions taken by the military outside Britain will later be found to be subject to challenge under the ECHR.'[29]

The deluge of cases brought against the British government from the period of occupation in Iraq was so great that it had to create a special Iraq Historic Allegations Team (IHAT) in the MOD. They investigated over three thousand cases, and found many to be based on false allegations. A British solicitor was struck off by the profession's Disciplinary Tribunal in 2017 for professional misconduct[30] and by the time IHAT was wound up in June 2017, the caseload had fallen to around twenty. In announcing this, Defence Secretary Michael Fallon added: 'We are taking steps to make sure that the reputation of our Armed Forces cannot be attacked in this dishonest way again.'[31] Boris Johnson's government finally introduced draft legislation in 2020[32] to require all future governments to consider derogating from the ECHR in relation to significant overseas military operations. The purpose was also to give members of the armed forces greater certainty that the realities of military operations would be taken into account when deciding on prosecutions for alleged offences. The measures include a presumption that any prosecution would be exceptional if more than five years had elapsed from the date of an incident, and that the agreement of the Attorney General would be necessary before such a prosecution could take place.

The scale of resources required to investigate the Iraq claims, the cloud of uncertainty this created for many former members of the armed services, and the evidence that the whole process was open to widespread manipulation show how poorly adapted human rights law is to regulating military campaigns. The legislation aims to reduce the likelihood of this particular problem happening again. But the risk that actions on the battlefield could one way or another land up being scrutinized under provisions of human rights law will be another reason for caution on the part of ministers and their advisers about using the military instrument.

This constraint seems to apply disproportionately to Britain, given the wide scope its system of judicial review provides to bring cases against the government. Other countries have different legal traditions. For example, US legislation excludes or severely limits the scope to bring legal cases against individual members of the armed force, and French courts show much greater deference to their governments' decisions on national security issues than is the case in the UK. Forty-seven countries are signatories to the ECHR, including Russia. All are therefore subject to its provisions in principle, although it is hard to imagine families of members of the Russian armed forces trying to claim damages from their government on behalf of their loved ones killed in military operations.

Military power and foreign policy

For all the constraints on using the armed forces, Britain has not suddenly become pacifist. The armed forces rightly enjoy a high reputation for their professionalism and effectiveness. Opinion polls suggest that there is still a majority in favour of maintaining a strong defence, but that the public are, understandably, much more wary about how it is used. One poll in 2013 showed that 31 per cent of respondents thought that the armed forces should intervene abroad when other people's freedoms were threatened, while 44 per cent thought they should do so only when British interests were threatened, and 21 per cent only when British territory was threatened.[33]

This is borne out in the way the armed forces are actually being used. Following the withdrawal of the last combat troops from Afghanistan, the only operations have been conducted by the RAF. British jets played a leading part in the US-led air campaign against ISIS in Iraq and Syria from 2014. Prime Minister Theresa May approved cruise missile strikes against Syrian military targets in 2017 in a joint action with the US and France, after a further use of chemical weapons. She did not ask for prior parliamentary approval and so reasserted the valuable prerogative of a British prime minister to decide on military action in cases of real urgency, and to inform Parliament after the event. But apart from air strikes, the only international activities of the British armed forces have been at the low-risk end of the spectrum: training and mentoring missions, non-combat peacekeeping and naval anti-piracy patrols, and assisting the government at home on the Olympics and emergencies such as floods and the pandemic.

The contrast with France – the only major Western military power which was not part of the Iraq coalition – is striking. Largely free from the Iraq effect, French public opinion has been more willing to accept the traditional interventionist approach in the francophone countries of the Sahel and West Africa. When Islamist terrorist groups threatened to depose the government in Mali in 2013, the Bamako government asked for urgent French support. President Francois Hollande, a socialist politician who was far from being a hawk on military issues, nonetheless followed traditional French practice by deploying significant forces for what proved to be a dangerous and prolonged counter-insurgency operation in the difficult conditions of the Sahara desert. It involved fierce fighting which France sustained with little combat support from other allies.

The French operation prevented an Islamist takeover of this weak country, which would have destabilized the whole region. The verdict of French public opinion was broadly positive on an operation which was seen to have safeguarded a region crucial to French interests and to have shown the prowess of the French armed forces. As the operation dragged on into its seventh year with a continuing toll of military casualties, some French commentators began to speak of France's Afghanistan. For all that, the French commitment to Mali, and the smaller operations they have mounted to support governments in French-speaking

Africa, for example in the Central African Republic in 2014, have made France the dominant Western power in a region where Europe has substantial security interests in countering terrorism and illegal migration.

The West's adversaries, particularly Russia, continue to see the use of military force, overtly or in ambiguous ways, as an integral part of their foreign policy. The Russian military interventions in Georgia in 2008 and in Ukraine in 2014 confirmed Russia as the main power broker in Central Asia and the Caucasus. While the West debated indirect support to the Syrian rebels in 2012–13, it was Putin who took the risk of putting boots on the ground (or rather several squadrons of fighter-bombers and the two thousand or so personnel to support them) in an intervention which helped to tilt the direction of the civil war in Assad's favour. By 2019, with some ground forces deployed in Northern Syria as well, Putin was in a position to arbitrate a ceasefire between Turkish and Kurdish forces after the Turkish incursion in north-east Syria. Russia is now the dominant power in the area. It was Russia which brokered an end to the fighting which erupted in late 2020 between Armenia and Azerbaijan over the disputed enclave of Nagorno-Karabakh, and Russia which deployed peacekeepers to oversee the ceasefire. Putin has taken risks. By siding with Assad against the Sunni communities in Syria, he may stoke resentment among a new generation of Sunni Muslims in the southern provinces of Russia on the model of the Chechen uprising of the 1990s. But, in the short term, he has chosen to use his military forces decisively for foreign-policy effect.

The era of large-scale Western interventions followed by long periods trying to prop up weak local regimes is over. But there is no political consensus in Britain on how the country should now use its military power to safeguard its interests. The experience since the end of the Cold War has shown how vital it is to set clear and attainable objectives for any military action, and how hard it is to use military power to achieve foreign-policy goals. George H. W. Bush showed how it could be done, defining a limited objective for the 1990 Gulf War (the expulsion of Iraqi forces from Kuwait) and achieving it. The interventions in Bosnia and Kosovo, which the Major and Blair governments played such a prominent part in, were aimed at ending massive human rights abuses. In my view, Western action was justified, and at least partially successful – and European countries have stuck at the task of supporting these countries in their painfully slow process of nation-building. Afghanistan began as a counter-terrorism response to the unprovoked 9/11 attacks, and Britain had a strong national interest in joining her closest ally in an operation designed to prevent further mass terrorist attacks. But the rationale for sending a British brigade to Helmand Province in 2004 was much less clear, and the heavy casualties sustained over the following decade were correspondingly hard to explain to the public.

Blair's decision to join the Americans in a military campaign in Iraq, with its fateful consequences, has been exhaustively examined in the report of the Chilcot Inquiry published in 2016. Blair was clearly wrong to have committed to Bush in secret in April 2002 to join him in military action 'come what may', long before he and his Cabinet had weighed up all the risks and considered the scale of what the US, Britain and other members of the coalition would be taking on as occupying powers. Blair's early commitment to supporting the invasion gave him very little influence on the key decisions which shaped the military campaign and the ensuing occupation. British plans were constantly disrupted by changes of mind in Washington, in particular the decision in the weeks leading up to the outbreak of hostilities in 2003 to switch post-conflict arrangements from the State Department to the Pentagon.

The flawed decision-making on Iraq led Cameron to put Whitehall on notice as soon as he became Leader of the Opposition in 2005 that, if elected, he intended to introduce a National Security Council (NSC), based loosely on the American system. When as prime minister he had to work out what to do about the looming massacre of anti-Gaddafi demonstrators in Libya in 2011, he used this NSC machinery to ensure a much more disciplined decision-making process than Blair's on Iraq. As we have seen, the initial objective of avoiding a significant loss of life in Benghazi was achieved. But once again, ending the operation proved much harder than starting it, and without forces on the ground, the coalition had little influence over the factional fighting which developed as soon as the Gaddafi regime fell.

British and American politicians are now instinctively averse to boots on the ground. NATO has been shaken by the US shift away from leadership in managing international crises. The EU is divided on whether even to try to turn itself into a military power. The pendulum has swung a long way from Blair's readiness to use armed force as an instrument of his foreign policy. As the Harvard historian Professor Joe Nye put it in his book *The Future of Power*, 'Force is more costly and more difficult for most states to use than in the past.'[34] That is particularly true for democracies.

It is a good thing that the bar is now set very high in terms of deploying British armed forces into combat. That should always be a last resort. But this approach has consequences in a world where potential adversaries like Russia are much less inhibited about using military power to achieve their foreign-policy goals.

The UK, as it sets out on an independent foreign policy, is in particular need of finding new ways to use its military power as an instrument of foreign policy.

PART II

What to Do Now

4

PICKING THE RIGHT THREATS

The expanding universe of national security

Wider still and wider shall thy bounds be set.
From *Land of Hope and Glory* by A. C. Benson[1]

Getting the terrorist threat in proportion

On the afternoon of 11 September 2001, I was with the British Foreign Secretary Jack Straw, the Defence Secretary Geoff Hoon and the Chief of Defence Staff, Admiral Sir Mike Boyce, in the high Victorian splendour of Straw's office overlooking St James's Park, when one of the Private Secretaries called us out to watch the television. Thick black smoke was billowing from one of the twin towers of the World Trade Center in New York. Our first assumption was that there had been a terrible accident. Then we watched in horror as an airliner headed straight for the second tower and hit with a sickening impact.

Within an hour, two further airliners had crashed, one into the Pentagon in Washington. There was no longer any doubt that we were facing a terrorist attack on an unimaginable scale. Our suspicions immediately turned to al-Qaida. After all, they had a track record of audacious attacks against American targets, most dramatically the suicide bombings at the US embassies in Kenya and Tanzania, which killed 224 people, including twelve

Americans. As Chairman of the Joint Intelligence Committee, I had produced assessments of al-Qaida's responsibility for the bombing of the USS *Cole* in Aden harbour in 2000 which had killed seventeen US sailors. But what was happening in front of our eyes in the US was on a totally different scale and had obviously involved elaborate planning over many months. How had the intelligence community failed to pick up any trace of the plotters? And suppose the New York attacks were part of an even wider assault on Western targets? At this point in our speculations, Hoon looked at Boyce and said, 'We'd better get back to the MOD and see to the air defence of London.' A sobering thought.

When they had gone, there was a pause before Straw and I embarked on a whirl of diplomatic activity, coordinating the UK's response with friends and allies around the world to translate the outpouring of solidarity with the US into practical measures. In that pause, the words of a previous Foreign Secretary, Edward Grey, came back to me. As he looked out from those same windows into the gathering dusk in August 1914, he saw the gas lamps being lit and mused, 'the lamps are going out all over Europe; we shall not see them lit again in our lifetime.' We were not facing anything comparable to a world war, but the phrase seemed to capture the sense we all had that this was a moment when everything changed.

Whatever their precise motives, the terrorists demolished not only the World Trade Center, but also the American assumption that the primary threats to them came from other states. The point did not need to be explicit when Roosevelt, Truman and the US Congress developed the concept of national security. The experience of their generation was that the risks they faced were the capabilities and ambitions of totalitarian adversaries.

Even after the Soviet threat evaporated, the habit of identifying foreign leaders as public enemies continued, and the easier they were to caricature for American public opinion the better. The Ayatollahs in Iran, Saddam Hussein, Gaddafi and Milošević all took their turn.

What 9/11 showed was that the American homeland could be attacked by a little-known terrorist group operating from the caves of Afghanistan. It was a particularly traumatic experience for a nation grown accustomed to its continental invulnerability in the sixty years since Pearl Harbor. Given the level of public alarm and the far-reaching political consequences of a further attack on the scale of 9/11, countering terrorism became the paramount security objective for successive US administrations over the following fifteen years.

The attacks shifted the balance in US domestic policy away from individual freedom and towards security, as all travellers to US airports will know. The overriding urgency of preventing further similar attacks also had a darker side. The US Congress gave the President sweeping powers including indefinite detention of suspected terrorists anywhere in the world. The new law also extended the practice – which had begun under the Clinton presidency – of bringing terrorist suspects to the US for trial, to cover 'extraordinary rendition', that is, forcibly taking suspects to detention centres such as Guantanamo Bay.

The British Parliament's Intelligence and Security Committee investigated the role of British intelligence agencies in this draconian American programme. They found that British personnel had not been involved in physical mistreatment, but were nevertheless strongly critical that those involved had not raised concerns about the mistreatment of detainees by some of their American colleagues. The Committee recognized their dilemma – the detainees were a significant source of information which could possibly prevent other large-scale terrorist attacks in the UK. The interrogations were conducted by Americans in an American facility. The British agents therefore had little influence on the proceedings. They had a difficult balancing act as 'the junior partner with limited access or influence, and distinctly uncomfortable at the prospect of complaining to their host'.[2]

The attacks of 2001 brought domestic and international security together in a frightening way. Like those of us standing around Straw's TV screen, governments and publics across the Western world understood immediately that they were as much a target for al-Qaida terrorism as the US, and that improving international counter-terrorism cooperation was vital. Terrorist attacks on civilian targets were not a new phenomenon in Europe. The UK and Spain had lived with the long and bloody campaigns mounted by terrorist groups pursuing independence for their regions – the IRA in Ireland and ETA in the Basque region of Spain. Germany had suffered the far left terrorism of the Baader–Meinhof Gang. But these groups committed their terrorist acts in pursuit of identifiable political objectives. They could be dealt with as a domestic security problem. The IRA and ETA campaigns were eventually abandoned after political agreements. The al-Qaida threat was different. It left national security communities scrambling for ways to counter determined attackers willing to die in the process of killing as many innocent civilians as possible.

The attack on the London transport system in July 2005, which left fifty-two people dead and many injured, introduced a further new dimension to this threat. The London terrorists were not a group of hardened fighters smuggled in from Afghanistan, but young men born and raised in the UK. They had shown no prior signs of radicalization and, although two had visited Pakistan, there was no evidence that they were controlled from abroad. The official report into the bombings concluded that 'the process of indoctrinating these men seems to have been through personal contact and group bonding.'[3] This was a home-grown threat. It forced all of us in the UK national security community to change radically the way we worked. Civil servants who had spent their lives working on foreign policy or intelligence found themselves sitting round the same table as specialists on community cohesion, education and the oversight of mosques and prisons as we looked for effective ways of spotting early signs that individuals might be turning to violence, and of promoting alternative messages about the peaceful nature of Islam. Plots could only be spotted and foiled before they led to death on the streets of Britain by much more effective working across the whole of government. This approach was even given a name in the 2018 National Security Capability Review[4] – the 'fusion doctrine'.

The French authorities were a shade complacent after the London attacks. They had long looked askance at British acceptance of large ethnic communities which maintained their own cultures and practices. They saw the UK as more tolerant of militants, sometimes referring acidly to 'Londonistan'. The French doctrine was that immigrants were expected to assimilate and adopt French ways of living. It was unthinkable that a French gendarme should wear a Sikh turban or a Muslim woman a burqa in public. The very word 'community', which in English has a reassuring, inclusive ring, becomes '*communitarisme*' in French, with a highly pejorative sense close to ghettoization. The French flattered themselves that what they thought were much more assimilated immigrant communities would not produce the sort of home-grown terrorism which London suffered. That changed with the spate of attacks which began when Mohammed Merah, who had grown up on a bleak housing estate outside Toulouse, killed seven people in the city in 2012, and culminated in the assault on the Stade de France and Bataclan theatre in Paris in 2015, which left 130 people dead. Since then, Britain and France have worked much more closely together, each recognizing the need for more effective deradicalization programmes.

The scale of the problem for Britain, France and other countries has increased further with the return of several thousand European citizens who had been drawn to fight for ISIS in Syria and Iraq. Security services face the problem of prioritizing their limited surveillance capacities, making choices that run the risk that some attack planning will go undetected. And the threat is constantly changing. The leaders of the ISIS terrorist group have largely been forced out of their base in Syria and have dispersed to other areas where weak governments give them scope to operate, such as the Sahel region. Continued refugee flows give these groups opportunities to insert radicalized individuals into European countries with a view to carrying out attacks one day. Tactics have also changed. Terrorist groups have learned that elaborate planning involving extensive communication is likely to be detected, so the trend has been towards smaller-scale attacks with minimal preparation. Since guns, and particularly automatic weapons, are hard to get hold of in Britain, would-be terrorists are resorting to using vehicles or kitchen knives to inflict casualties.

The random nature of terrorist attacks makes them particularly terrifying and attracts far more media coverage than other forms of violent crime. The destruction of New York's World Trade Center was a dramatic enough event to change thinking about national security and the balance between security and liberty across the Western world. If al-Qaida had succeeded in laying their hands on nuclear, chemical or biological weapons in some form, as they were apparently seeking to do in the years after 9/11, they could have had an even more dramatic impact. But in the event, the scale of resources put into intelligence work and international cooperation on counter-terrorism since 2001 has successfully reduced the threat to the point where it can now be treated as a serious law and order problem, not an existential threat to any Western nation.

George W. Bush's 'War on Terror' slogan was an instinctive response to the anger and fear felt in the immediate aftermath of the 2001 attacks. But it was bad strategy. It gave the terrorists a spurious credibility as adversaries in a war. When terrorists made the mistake of acting like states, holding territory as ISIS did briefly in Syria after 2014, they were indeed defeated on the battlefield. The goal of defeating terrorism – repeated endlessly by political leaders after each subsequent terrorist atrocity – is however simply not possible. The risk of another spectacular attack cannot be reduced to zero. But the overall level of deaths from terrorism in Western Europe is now far lower than the 400 a year at the height of the IRA and ETA campaigns in the 1970s and 1980s. Even in years of multiple Islamist attacks, such as 2015, there were 150 deaths from terrorism in EU countries. By 2019, this had fallen to ten.[5] In the same year, 132 people were killed in knife-crime attacks in London, with a similar total in 2019. The death rate from terrorism has fallen even more dramatically in the US since 9/11. On average, two people per year have been killed by terrorists in the US since 2001, as against sixty-nine by lawnmowers and almost 11,500 by gun-wielding Americans.[6]

The terrorism threat is a good example of both the need to adjust security priorities from time to time, and the difficulty of doing so. The threat of attacks either by Islamist or extreme-right terrorists will remain for the long term. But two decades after 9/11, the dedicated work of well-resourced intelligence and law enforcement agencies has succeeded in mitigating the risk, particularly of large-scale attacks, even though it cannot ever be eliminated. The level of public anxiety about terrorism now bears no relation to the objective risk to any individual being caught up in a terrorist event.

Recalibrating public attitudes to the terrorist threat needs political leadership, particularly after an attack. Jacinda Arden, prime minister of New Zealand, did just that by resolutely refusing to use the name of the right-wing extremist who killed fifty people in attacks on mosques in Christchurch in March 2019. The British authorities rightly emphasized the criminal backgrounds of the perpetrators of a series of small-scale knife attacks in London in 2019–20, and responded by changing the law to intervene in the early release from prison of those who presented a continued threat. Treating the terrorism issue as a long-term law and order problem, and the issue of radicalization as something to be dealt with primarily by social policy, creates some space to concentrate political energies on the risks and threats which could have much greater impact on the country and its citizens.

National security inflation

The paradox of Britain's national security policy is that, in the fifteen years after 2001, it had both too few and too many priorities. In practice, two issues dominated the agenda: the wars of intervention and preventing terrorist attacks. At the same time, other threats and hazards accumulated, lists of priorities lengthened, but governments struggled to spot the really important emerging issues. This paradox goes a long way to explain why Britain (like other Western countries) was caught unawares by the re-emergence of great power competition, and unprepared for the Covid-19 pandemic.

The process of national security inflation has been under way since the end of the Cold War. That event lifted the threat of nuclear annihilation and freed up governments to attend to other aspects of the safety and security of their citizens. The US has published National Security Strategy (NSS) documents since the 1980s, which track the expanding universe of national security as successive administrations added to their catalogue the latest issue causing public concern. When Gordon Brown's government issued Britain's first NSS in 2008, this was focused heavily on counter-terrorism, but also made the case to a British audience for a wider view:

> . . .over recent decades, our view of national security has broadened to include threats to individual citizens and to our way of life, as well as to the integrity and interests of the state. That is why this strategy deals with transnational crime, pandemics and flooding – not part of the traditional idea of national security, but clearly challenges that can affect large numbers of our citizens. . .

The fact that the domain of national security was expanding, with more government departments involved and a growing need for prioritization, was one of the main reasons behind Cameron's decision to create a National Security Council. The Conservative Party worked up their ideas for this while in opposition, drawing heavily on the American model, though on a much smaller scale.

Their thinking emphasized the importance of an 'all hazards' approach, including improved readiness to deal with natural disasters and other unforeseen emergencies.

A national security apparatus, like any other part of government, reflects the style and interests of the leader. David Cameron asked me to become the UK's first National Security Adviser and to set up his new NSC. In fact he had made a campaign pledge that it would meet on his first day in office. With a scramble, we achieved that, and learned a lot about how Cameron wanted his new body to work. He broke with the tradition that British Cabinet Committees were composed entirely of ministers, by insisting that the government's most senior advisers on national security issues – the Chief of Defence Staff (CDS), the Chairman of the Joint Intelligence Committee (JIC) and the heads of the three intelligence agencies, as well as the National Security Adviser – should always attend.

The Cameron approach was to avoid groupthink by encouraging frank debate between the ministers and advisers in order to question assumptions and to challenge official advice. He always enjoyed it when in the process he unearthed disagreements between Whitehall departments which had been carefully glossed over in papers prepared for the meeting. He demanded that the NSC meet every week, that senior ministers should attend and that it would make decisions on a wide range of security-related issues. As a result, the group of ministers who formed the first NSC rapidly developed a familiarity with subjects ranging well beyond their departmental briefs, which put them in a good position to make cross-cutting judgements on priorities.

The NSC also gave the heads of the British intelligence agencies regular contact with senior ministers collectively for the first time ever. Since the war, each intelligence agency has had its own supervising minister: the Foreign Secretary for the Secret Intelligence Service (SIS) and the Government Communications Headquarters (GCHQ), and the Home Secretary for the Security Service. The NSC gave them a forum for a regular exchange with the prime minister and the key group of ministers coordinating national security policy. This has allowed the intelligence community to feed their analysis and judgements directly into the policymaking process, while respecting the principle that they do not themselves make policy proposals.

Cameron's NSC was good at doing but less good at reflecting. To help the new team set priorities, my team and I decided to conduct a systematic assessment of all the many disruptive risks we could think of which were large enough in scale or potential impact to need action from the government. We assembled a long list and then weighed up for each one the likelihood of the risk materializing over a five- to twenty-year period and the impact if it did. On the basis of this matrix, we identified fifteen top risks and divided them further into three Tiers, with those that scored most highly on likelihood and impact in Tier One.

Like any horizon-scanning process, it was imperfect and ultimately subjective. Some of the potential risks, such as nuclear, biological or chemical weapons attack were low likelihood but so cataclysmic in their potential impact that they had to figure prominently on a list of risks, and to involve vastly expensive mitigation strategies including the nuclear deterrent force. For all its imperfections, our proposed ranking of risks at least obliged ministers in the NSC to focus on risk management of the most dire threats facing the country. We published the prioritized list of fifteen top threats in the National Security Strategy[7] in October 2010, at the same time as the Strategic Defence and

Security Review[8] and a review of spending which set budgets for all Whitehall departments for five years. The Coalition government was criticized for rushing this very wide-ranging suite of documents through in five months. But it was only by taking decisions at the same time on risk priorities, policies to respond to them and the necessary funding allocations that the government could claim to be making a genuine strategy which aligned ends, ways and means.

The list of fifteen top risks which we published in 2010 was as follows:

Tier One

- International terrorism affecting the UK or its interests, including a chemical, biological, radiological and nuclear attack by terrorists; and/or a significant increase in the levels of terrorism relating to Northern Ireland.

- Hostile attacks upon UK cyber space by other states and large-scale cyber crime.

- A major accident or natural hazard which requires a national response, such as severe coastal flooding affecting three regions of the UK, or an influenza pandemic.

- An international military crisis between states, drawing in the UK and its allies, as well as other states and non-state actors.

Tier Two

- An attack on the UK or its Overseas Territories by another state or proxy using chemical, biological, radiological or nuclear weapons.

- The risk of major instability, insurgency or civil war overseas which creates an environment that terrorists can exploit and threaten the UK.

- A significant increase in the level of organised crime affecting the UK.

- Severe disruption to information received, transmitted or collected by satellites, possibly as the result of a deliberate attack by another state.

Tier Three

- A large-scale conventional military attack on the UK by another state (not involving the use of chemical, biological, radiological and nuclear weapons) resulting in fatalities and damage to infrastructure within the UK.

- A significant increase in the level of terrorists, organised criminals, illegal immigrants and illicit goods across the UK border to enter the UK.

- Disruption to oil or gas supplies to the UK, or price instability, as a result of war, accident, major political upheaval or deliberate manipulation of supply by producers.

- A major release of radioactive material from a civil nuclear site within the UK which affects one or more regions.

- A conventional attack by a state on another NATO or EU member to which the UK would have to respond.

- An attack on a UK Overseas Territory as a result of a sovereignty dispute or a wider regional conflict.

- Short- to medium-term disruption to international supplies of resources (e.g. food, minerals) essential to the UK.

Obeying the inexorable law that all government priority lists grow over time, when the NSS was revised in 2015, it increased the overall number of top risks to twenty, with six in the Tier One category.

National security inflation will continue. Real security comes from regularly reassessing the relative likelihood and impact of risks, taking account of the effectiveness of steps to mitigate them, and retiring issues which are no longer pressing. Without that, NSS documents grow by sedimentation and become exercises in false reassurance. The public is promised that governments have all the problems in hand but, in practice, resources are finite and not everything can be top priority. The 2010 list of priorities was an accurate reflection of the risks as they stood at that time, but the world has moved on a long way since then. The consequences for Britain of the changing geometry of power and specifically of the growing US–China confrontation will need constant attention from the National Security Council in years to come.

Another issue which was already in our Tier One risks in 2010 but which will grow in importance in the coming decades is resilience against the most serious disruptive events: a massive cyber attack disrupting vital services, climate change and its impact on global stability, and most pressing of all, further threats to public health.

The problem of resilience

The 2010 risk assessment showed the importance of building resilience against cyber attacks aimed at critical national infrastructure. Cyber defence is not something the government alone can deliver. It needs a partnership between the government, businesses and citizens. Fortunately, as this issue increased in urgency, the British government could turn to its world-class signals intelligence agency, GCHQ, to lead its work on strengthening cyber resilience. Their code-breaking skills turned out to be very relevant to this field, which was increasingly being exploited by criminals as well as adversary states like Russia, China, Iran and North Korea. In a powerful symbol of new ways of working between the intelligence world and the rest of society, GCHQ set up in 2016 the National Cyber Security Centre (NCSC) in a glass-fronted office building across the road from Victoria station in London. Its task was to put out guidance and alerts on the latest cyber threats to all users of the internet, from the most sophisticated corporate clients to individuals on their home computers. The NCSC has shown considerable creativity in overcoming the traditional barriers to sharing intelligence-based information with businesses and the public. And they have brought into sharp focus the real nature of the threat.

In an illuminating analogy, the former head of the NCSC, Ciaran Martin, described the cyber weapons used by states and criminals as like a virus: 'They look for a host. They spread. They enter the environment, and it's not always easy to predict, and sometimes even harder to control, how they will behave.'[9] Martin noted that the two most damaging recent cyber attacks were launched in 2017 by North Korea (to extort money from businesses in Asia) and Russia (against a specific company in Ukraine). Both went viral by accident, causing damage and disruption to businesses and individuals round the world at random. It follows from this that the best form of defence against cyber attacks is not to threaten counter attacks (releasing our own viruses into the cyber environment) but to improve resilience: designing cyber security into new hardware and software (which might be thought of as a vaccine), raising awareness among all users of the necessary hygiene by keeping their basic protections up to date, alerting against the latest threat.

After the Cold War, successive UK governments also started to give more attention to risks which were not posed by human adversaries and could not therefore be deterred by military means or pre-empted by intelligence, diplomacy or police work. They came from natural disasters, which have the potential to disrupt the fragile balance of modern societies dependent on complex global supply chains and just-in-time delivery for essential goods of all kinds.

The first time I realized the extent of this vulnerability was when I arrived in the Cabinet Office to take over the role of Chairman of the Joint Intelligence Committee in September 2000 to find Blair and his government totally fixated on a sudden crisis over fuel stocks, caused by the blockade of the country's few refineries by protesters against the level of fuel duty. Within forty-eight hours, panic was in the air as long queues of motorists formed outside petrol stations which had run dry, and hospitals were running short of supplies. Blair comments in his memoirs that he failed to act soon enough because he had not understood how quickly any interruption in fuel supplies would bring the country to a halt.[10]

The fuel blockade, and the outbreak of foot-and-mouth disease which preceded it, raised awareness in Whitehall of the whole issue of resilience. That is why the 2010 NSS made a major accident or natural hazard one of the four top tier risks. The accompanying narrative highlighted the potential disruptive effect of an influenza pandemic. It drew attention to the fact that these had happened four times in the previous century, most recently with the 2009 H1N1 swine flu outbreak, adding:

> The most notable influenza pandemic of the last century occurred in 1918–19 and is often referred to as the 'Spanish flu'. It caused an estimated 20–40 million deaths worldwide with an estimated 228,000 in the UK alone. While the outbreak of swine flu last year, which resulted in 457 deaths, did not match the severity of the worst-case scenario that we plan for, future pandemic influenza outbreaks could be much more serious. There is a high probability of another influenza pandemic occurring, and, based on a range of data, possible impacts of a future pandemic could be that up to one half of the UK population becomes infected, resulting in between 50,000–75,000 deaths in the UK, with corresponding disruption to everyday life.[11]

In the 2015 NSS, this area was given even greater prominence as a separate risk entitled 'Public Health: a major human health crisis'. Yet Britain was caught woefully unprepared for the Covid-19 virus which swept the world with such devastating speed in 2020.

Why did the clear signals in the 2010 and 2015 National Security Strategies not trigger more effective resilience preparations? The full answer will take time to emerge. But there is enough already in the public domain to shed some light on why successive governments failed to be ready for the risk of a pandemic. The story also sheds light on the wider problem of persuading busy ministers to give attention to future-proofing society against risks that are possible, even likely, but uncertain – they might happen next week, or next year, or never.

The first reason the government was caught short was that, as this chapter has discussed, the lion's share of ministerial time and extra funding for a decade or more after 9/11 went on the most pressing and immediate security issues of fighting terrorism and conducting large-scale military operations. These urgent crisis management priorities sucked up energy that could have been applied to the potential crises over the horizon.

Secondly, the pandemic risk was followed up after the 2010 NSS, but never to the point of spending serious money. The Cabinet Office Civil Contingencies Unit was responsible for progress-chasing across Whitehall to ensure that contingency planning was done on each of the risks on the priority list. They evidently did their work, since in 2011 the Department of Health published the UK Influenza Pandemic Preparedness Strategy.[12] This is typical of a government strategy document. It is long (seventy pages), meticulous in describing the problem, and honest about the risk that things could get very bad:

> Local planners should prepare to extend capacity on a precautionary but reasonably practicable basis, and aim to cope with a population mortality rate of up to 210,000 – 315,000 additional deaths, possibly over

> as little as a 15 week period and perhaps half of these
> over three weeks at the height of the outbreak.

But the imagination of the drafters seems to have failed when it came to the practical implications of a crisis involving deaths on anything like that scale. The document was reassuring that the government had stockpiles of face masks and respirators for medical workers, but it did not foresee the need for huge numbers of ventilators or the intensive care beds to go with them. There were no operational conclusions for taking any action that would cost money. Instead, the authors took refuge from a contingency too awful to contemplate by setting up a further review to ensure that the costs of preparing for the unpredictable were justified against the risk. No decision to invest money was taken.

In other words, the response to the risk of a pandemic set out in the NSS was to produce a strategy, and establish a process to consider the implications. Other plans followed, in 2012, and 2014. But when the government held an influenza pandemic exercise in 2016 codenamed Cygnus, it was clear that, despite the strategy papers, resilience against a reasonable worst-case pandemic had not improved. The government did not publish the conclusions of the exercise, but the then Chief Medical Officer, Sally Davies, said publicly: 'We've just had in the UK a three-day exercise on flu, on a pandemic that killed a lot of people. It became clear that we could not cope with the excess bodies.'[13] She added that one of the problems was an inadequate number of ventilators. But even this did not lead to the stockpiling of that essential piece of equipment or any other expansion of capacity. A pandemic was a known risk but of unknown timing or severity, and there were always higher priorities for hard-pressed NHS staff and budgets.

This is a key point for improving resilience planning for pandemics or any other hazard. Senior political figures live in a world fraught with risks of every kind. They could wake up tomorrow morning to find they are out of a job in a sudden reshuffle. A political scandal could pitch the government into turmoil. Something in their past could come back to haunt them. There could be a terrorist attack, a devastating flood, a strike by fuel tanker drivers. Or a pandemic. The way most seem to cope – and this is no doubt true in other stressful occupations – is to concentrate on the immediate crisis and not to spend time worrying about the myriad disruptive things which could happen, but might not. One senior medical adviser commented that pandemic preparation involved 'telling governments what they don't want to know, to spend money they don't have, on something they don't think will happen'.

The pandemic crisis has changed the world far more fundamentally than 9/11 did. Just as massive resources were pumped into intelligence and law enforcement after the 2001 attacks, so governments are greatly increasing spending to improve the readiness of health systems to cope with the next threat. But a key lesson of the pandemic crisis is that resilience has to be about more than coping with today's crisis. That needs a change of mindset across government. The wrong reaction to the pandemic would be to focus future resilience work largely on public health, at the expense of other risks which could have devastating consequences at some point in the future, in particular climate change.

Picking the right threats is an art not a science. Since the end of the Cold War, governments have had much more flexibility to choose their priorities; Britain's track record is mixed. The military interventions to avert humanitarian calamities or deny safe space to terrorist groups failed to achieve their strategic objectives more often than they succeeded. By contrast, the response to Islamist terrorism, one of the four top-tier risks we identified in the 2010 National Security Strategy, has been a real success. Not every plot has been foiled – that would be an impossible definition of success. But the fact that there has not been a successful attack on anything like the scale of 9/11 for twenty years, and that the numbers of deaths from terrorism are on a declining trend, is the result of relentless efforts by the intelligence and security communities, with Britain playing a leading part. Britain's response to the threat of cyber attack, another of the 2010 top-tier risks, has been one of the most effective in the world. But the rise in the threats from Russia and China did not get the attention it deserved from Western countries including Britain. They were heavily focused on immediate issues like the fight against Islamist terrorism and dealing with the migration crisis of 2015 and, in Britain's case, distracted by Brexit from 2016 onwards. And there was no effective follow-up to the high priority given in 2010 to the risk of a pandemic.

Britain now has the right tool in the NSC to enable the government to set priorities among the risks and threats facing the country, and to ensure that policy decisions are followed through into practical actions. Given the range of threats and risks faced by post-Brexit Britain, it was surprising to find that the NSC met only rarely in the first year of the Johnson government. Tools are of no use if they are left in the shed.

5

REVIVING THE LOST
ART OF STRATEGY

Why are British governments so
bad at longer-term thinking?

There is no longer such a thing as strategy,
there is only crisis management.[1]
Robert McNamara, 1962

Strategy and democracy

If you walk down Whitehall in London on the opposite side of
the road from Downing Street, you pass the white 1950s facade
of the Air Ministry, now the Ministry of Defence. Outside are
three imposing bronze statues of Britain's Second World War
military commanders. To the left and right are the warfighting
generals Montgomery of Alamein and Slim of Burma. To make
the point, Slim has binoculars slung around his neck. Between
them is their boss, the Chief of the Imperial General Staff and
chief military adviser to Churchill, Field Marshal Alan Brooke,
leaning back, as if gathering himself before hurrying to another
meeting across the road with the Prime Minister. On his plinth
are the simple words 'Master of Strategy'.

Although he is much less well known than the media-hungry Montgomery, Sir Alan Brooke (or Lord Alanbrooke as he became) deserves his central location and his accolade. He was the last of the truly great exponents in Britain of the art of strategy in wartime, the kind that has traditionally been called grand strategy. Churchill was capable of moments of sweeping grand strategic vision, and was unrivalled in his ability to find the words to bring a strategy to life. But he pursued with equal vigour what his biographer Andrew Roberts calls 'madcap schemes' and it was often Alanbrooke who had to ride him off them. As Roberts puts it, 'Brooke must take immense credit for steering Churchill off his favoured but flawed operations such as Jupiter (northern Norway) and Culverin (southern Sumatra).'[2]

The Yale professor John Lewis Gaddis defines grand strategy as 'the alignment of potentially unlimited aspirations with necessarily limited capabilities'.[3] That is a good description of Alanbrooke's particular gift as a strategist. It was the creative (sometimes explosive) tension between the vision of Churchill and the hard-headed judgement on the part of Alanbrooke and his Chiefs of Staff as to what Britain could do in practice that generated the successful British grand strategy during the Second World War.

The military historian Liddell Hart, writing in the 1960s, commented that

> the role of grand strategy – higher strategy – is to coordinate and direct all the resources of a nation. . . towards the attainment of the political object of the war. . . Furthermore, while the horizon of strategy is bounded by the war, grand strategy looks beyond the war to the subsequent peace.[4]

Churchill and Roosevelt were making grand strategy in Placentia Bay in 1941, and the statesmen of the late 1940s carried this through into the international structures of the post-war peace. Their capacity to think with strategic sweep as well as hard-headed pragmatism qualifies as grand strategy even by the demanding standards set by historians such as Hal Brands. He defined it as

> the theory, or logic, that binds a country's highest interests to its daily interactions with the world. . . grand strategy represents an integrated conception of interests, threats, resources, and policies. It is, in this sense, the intellectual architecture that gives structure to foreign policy and helps nations find their way in the world.[5]

The late 1940s were a high point of what the historian of war Lawrence Freedman calls, in another definition of strategy, 'the art of creating power'.[6] British statesmen used to be good at this. Harold Macmillan, who took on the premiership after the 1956 Suez debacle, soon sensed that far-reaching decisions were looming on Britain's relations with Europe, and with the United States approaching the end of the Eisenhower era. So in June 1959 he commissioned an eminent panel chaired by the Cabinet Secretary Norman Brook to

> try to forecast what the state of the world would be in 1970, and what role the United Kingdom would be able to play in it. I thought that if they had that picture before them, Ministers would be better able to formulate policies for the intervening years which would allow us to continue to play a significant part in world affairs.[7]

Brook and his group of military chiefs and senior civil servants delivered their Future Policy Study in February 1960.[8] Its fifty pages came closer than any other document that I saw over my forty years as a civil servant to a statement of grand strategy.[9] Helped by the fact that their report was top secret, the authors gave ministers an unvarnished assessment of Britain's economic outlook. They concluded that even if the country achieved the government's ambitious growth target of 2.8 per cent a year over the decade, 'our relative position vis-à-vis both the United States and Western Europe will nevertheless decline.'

Even though the panel were not tasked with policy conclusions, they left their readers in no doubt about the consequences for Britain of what was happening in Europe:

> The European Economic Community is of immense potential importance. . . if they continue to grow at their recent pace they will approach and perhaps reach the United States level by 1970. If therefore the 'Six' achieve a real measure of integration, a new world power will have come on the scene. . . It would probably replace us as the second member of the North Atlantic Alliance. . . there would be a considerable danger that other European countries would jump on the EEC bandwagon, and if an economic division led to conflict, the United States with their traditional attachment to the idea of European unity, might even feel obliged to support the Six against us, to the great detriment of Anglo-American cooperation.

The closing phrase showed that, as good civil servants, they had not lost their capacity for understatement, but the message was unmistakeable. The same was true of another point which the Study hammered home – the vital importance to Britain of the NATO alliance and of good cooperation with the US, and what was needed to secure that. In a message that still has salience today, they warned that 'Anglo-American partnership is not a law of nature' and Britain would need to show that it was capable of giving second place to its own interests in order to show that it was contributing to wider US objectives:

> If disputes or tensions force them to choose between their allies, they are likely to throw their weight behind the ally for whom they have most respect as an actively powerful opponent of Russian and Chinese expansionism, and as a large contributor to the joint aims of the free world. The continued intimacy of Anglo-American cooperation will only be possible provided that we can satisfy these conditions. . .

Bringing these two themes together, the authors produced a classic definition of British post-war strategy:

> One basic rule of British policy is clear: we must not find ourselves in a position of having to make a final choice between the United States and Europe. It would not be compatible with our vital interests to reject either one or the other, and the very fact that the choice was needed would mean the destruction of the Atlantic alliance.

This powerful study was not left to gather dust in the Cabinet Secretary's safe. Macmillan evidently brooded on it, understood the dangers it highlighted and, at the end of 1960, responded in a thirty-two-page memorandum known as the Grand Design. This set out his ambition 'to call attention to the need to organise the great forces of the free world – the USA, Britain and Europe – economically, politically and militarily, in a coherent effort to withstand the Communist tide all over the world'.

The historian Peter Hennessy gives a full account of the Grand Design in his book *Winds of Change*[10] and concludes that it would be 'hard to think of a subsequent premier who could have ranged so widely and thoughtfully with his or her own mind and pen'. Macmillan was making a sustained intellectual effort to turn grand strategy into operational policy. He aimed to satisfy the twin imperatives of the Future Policy Study by getting Britain into the European project and consolidating the special relationship with the US and John Kennedy, its new president. He failed on the first but succeeded on the second.

In one extraordinary week in December 1962, Macmillan started by meeting de Gaulle at a summit in Rambouillet, where the General finally made clear his opposition to British membership of the EEC at that time. His week ended with a meeting with Kennedy in Nassau at which they sealed the deal for Britain to buy the Polaris system, so linking the two countries together in an intense nuclear weapons cooperation which continues to this day. It took a further decade before Heath could complete the European campaign. But it was Norman Brook's study that set out the strategy, and also prepared the way for the progressive abandonment of pretensions to a global military role, leading to the decision by the Harold Wilson government later in the decade to withdraw from British military bases east of Suez.

Thatcher faced her grand strategic moment with the collapse of the Soviet empire in 1989. While a historic victory for the Western allies, it raised first-order questions about the future of

NATO, the impact on the process of European integration, and most urgently the issue of German unification. Events moved far too fast for a year-long exercise like the Future Policy Study. Even before the dramatic denouement on 9 November 1989, when East German border guards opened the gates in the Berlin Wall and watched as tens of thousands of their citizens flocked into West Berlin, the Foreign Office was beginning to think ahead. In a draft paper of 11 October, officials recommended: 'We cannot block reunification. . . The UK's best approach therefore is not to seek to discourage reunification but rather to exert influence over the speed and timing of any moves in that direction.'[11]

Sensible, pragmatic stuff. But it ran into the brick wall of Thatcher's opposition. The paper was never put to ministers because, as the British Ambassador to Moscow at the time, Sir Rodric Braithwaite, put it: 'The Prime Minister is highly allergic to allowing officials to think about German reunification.' It is always a bad sign when ministers stop civil servants thinking strategically about outcomes they dislike. Thatcher had dark forebodings of a united Germany not only dominating Europe economically but once again becoming a danger to its neighbours. She was also worried that moving too fast to a united Germany could destabilize Gorbachev, whose policies of opening up, or perestroika, had made the end of the Warsaw Pact possible. Pre-empting any strategic advice, Thatcher assured Gorbachev on her visit to Moscow on 22 September that 'Although NATO traditionally made statements supporting Germany's aspiration to be reunited, in practice we would not welcome it at all.'[12]

Thatcher's emotional response trapped her in the contradiction of welcoming victory in the Cold War and freedom for the countries of Eastern Europe, but opposing the choice of the people of East Germany – a single, united Germany. She was slower than other Western leaders to see where events were leading. George H. W. Bush supported Chancellor Helmut Kohl's accelerating drive for unification from the outset. President François Mitterrand was characteristically delphic, half-sharing Thatcher's fears, but in the end putting the Franco-German relationship above all else. Even Gorbachev came to terms with the inevitability of unification before Thatcher. So she was left stranded and had to execute a U-turn, which came at an FCO-organized seminar at Chequers on 27 January 1990. There, the Prime Minster finally accepted what her Foreign Secretary and all her advisers had been telling her – that the focus should not be on trying to stop unification but on a framework and timetable for handling unification. Taking a longer view, Thatcher's concerns about the impact of a rapid change in the European security order on the reform process in Russia turned out to be right. Putin has consolidated his power by exploiting the feelings of resentment that the West rode roughshod over Russian interests at a time when the country was weak. But her visceral dislike of German power left Britain sidelined during the largest upheaval in European security since 1945.

Macmillan rose to the challenge in 1960 and his twin-track approach of close relations with both Europe and America has guided British national strategy ever since. But in 1989, Thatcher was not prepared to set aside her prejudices and to test her instincts against new realities. She and her government were badly wrong-footed. The American and German leaders were the more effective strategists at the time.

Somewhere along the way since the 1940s, Western governments in general, but British governments in particular, have lost the art of long-term, comprehensive strategic planning. What is more, many politicians – at least in my experience – are not much interested in it. One British political leader (who had better remain nameless) once told me that when officials started to talk about strategy, he knew they wanted to stop him doing something. That is not to say that governments don't produce strategies. In fact, like all other organizations, they generate far too many so-called strategies to deliver every policy and to get out of every fix. But piling those up does not give you a coherent national strategy.

The inability of governments to think in broad terms about their place in the world seems to be a long-standing problem. McNamara had just resigned as US Defense Secretary in despair at US policy in Vietnam when he made the comments quoted at the head of this chapter to a congressional committee in 1962. Stephen Hadley, who served as George W. Bush's National Security Advisor, commented in a paper on the US NSC system in 2016 that successive US administrations from Kissinger's time onwards had been 'unsuccessful in incorporating deliberate forward-looking strategic level discussion and planning into the interagency process'.[13] Similar criticisms have been made of the British system. The Public Administration Select Committee (PASC) of the British House of Commons, reporting in 2010 on the British government's capacity for national strategy making, concluded in the case of Britain: 'We have all but lost the capacity to think strategically. We have simply fallen out of the habit and have lost the culture of strategy making. . . There is little idea of what the UK's national interest is, and therefore what our strategic purpose should be.'[14]

My point is not that this is something new, but that things are getting worse. Before substantiating that claim, it is worth making a distinction between what governments *say* about their national strategies, and what they actually *do*, which reveals their real strategic choices whether taken consciously or not. In democracies, all aspects of national security are permanently contested in the rough and tumble of the political process. Governments have to win public support for their approach, and then defend their policies against all comers. Published strategy papers are above all documents of political advocacy, not of dispassionate analysis. They are often couched at a safe level of generality. Here is a part of a section headed 'Our Values' from the UK's National Security Strategy of 2015:[15]

> The UK has a proud tradition of protecting its people, promoting civil liberties, upholding the rule of law and building diverse, integrated communities tolerant of different faiths and beliefs. Our democratic and inclusive values are the foundation of our security and prosperity. . . . Our long-term security and prosperity also depend on a stable international system that reflects our core British values: democracy, the rule of law, open, accountable governments and institutions, human rights, freedom of speech, property rights and equality of opportunity, including the empowerment of women and girls, are the building blocks of successful societies. They are part of the golden thread of conditions that lead to security and prosperity.

This is true, but so all-encompassing as to be of little use for the business of choosing priorities and allocating resources. Considerations like these have led some democratic countries with lively political cultures to decide not to publish national security policy papers at all. An example is Israel. The most recent historian of Israeli national security, Charles Freilich,[16] comments that not only has Israel never published such a document, but Israeli ministers avoid the policymaking processes that would be necessary to generate a strategy in the first place. This is because

> the very process itself conflicts with their political needs. In a highly politicised system, premiers, as well as defence and foreign ministers, do not wish to be bound by processes that require they present the Cabinet with a systematic analysis of Israel's objectives, and the optimal means of achieving them. Strategic clarity encourages divisions and puts political futures at risk. Ambiguity, conversely, can be constructive and is crucial to premiers' abilities to hold shaky coalitions together.

Freilich adds that the Israeli security establishment does of course produce numerous policy papers, but that they are 'overwhelmingly issue-specific and ad hoc, rather than being couched in a broad strategic construct'.

This points to the real problem. It is not that published strategy documents tend to be bland and full of clichés. The heart of the matter is that the pressures of modern democratic politics are making it harder for leaders to base what they *do* on careful thinking about the longer-term consequences of the options in front of them. Strategy involves making choices and politicians generally hate choosing. Choice involves risk and means winners and losers among political colleagues. It may well involve clarifying what has deliberately been kept ambiguous in order to bridge the gaps necessary to win elections or hold a coalition of interests together. Most politicians therefore prefer to put off difficult choices as long as possible, hoping that something will come up that will make the choice easier, or unnecessary. That applies particularly to issues of security which can have profound consequences for the well-being of their citizens.

It is why, for example, the thousands of French military forces who were deployed in the towns of France as a short-term measure after the terrorist attacks of 2015 were still there five years later. It was too risky to decide otherwise. Isabel Hardman, the author and journalist who made a detailed study of the conditions in which modern British politicians operate, accounted for their aversion to making choices in these terms:

> They avoid making decisions that, while necessary and urgent, will upset voters. They take decisions they don't need to in order to appear to be doing something about a problem that might not even exist. And they will do anything they can to get someone else who doesn't have to face those pesky elections to make a decision on their behalf.[17]

Modern political leaders suffer acutely from the tyranny of the immediate. They live under the relentless pressure of the 24/7 media cycle and the constant firehose of social media. Everyone wants instant responses. Leaving a damaging story without rebuttal even for a few hours means conceding the initiative to political opponents, or allowing fake news to gain a foothold. Under these pressures, the urgent and operational drives out the important. As Robert McNamara said, strategy is replaced with crisis management. Thinking about longer-term issues or underlying trends can seem a waste of time when the world is full of disruptive change. Keeping your job depends on dealing with the immediate crisis, not planning for something which may or may not happen in months or years.

All this is, I concede, a generalization. Some leaders are of course better than others at seeing the longer-term picture. Obama thought deeply about America's changing priorities and interests. In his bilateral meetings with Cameron which I attended, his approach was always rigorously analytical, his tone cool and professorial. He was determined to avoid the impulsive decision-making of his predecessor, to the point where he was often criticized for going too far in the other direction, allowing thinking to become a substitute for acting. His concept of a 'pivot to Asia' showed that he analysed correctly the way the tectonic plates were shifting. But it was not followed through into a significant change in the centre of gravity of US foreign policy. The 2013 decision to pull back from air strikes on Syrian chemical weapons sites caught his national security community by surprise as we have seen and was much criticized as a failure of resolve. Obama would say that it was a deliberate strategic choice, which set US policy on a different track.

France's President Emmanuel Macron also prides himself on a strategic approach to foreign policy. In 2020, he even revived the planning structure known as Le Plan. In the decades after 1945, this planning staff produced the five-year plans which helped to concentrate French industrial development in a few sectors and made the country a world leader, for example in high-speed trains and civil nuclear power. Macron explained that he wanted France to rediscover the sense of the long term and to make sure that government was not only about crisis management. This reflected his frustration at the difficulties in translating his strategic plans into real progress in reforming the rigidities of the French economic system. He found the same difficulty in trying to move the EU in the direction of further economic integration and greater capacity to project its power and influence in the world. Again, his ideas were powerful, but they did not find much resonance in other EU capitals. At that time, Germany's Chancellor Angela Merkel, a cautious politician who preferred to wait on events rather than shape them, was drawing towards the end of her long mandate. Britain and Italy were off the air, absorbed with internal politics. Other EU countries were giving priority to immediate concerns such as migration pressures or Russian intimidation. Macron offered his colleagues a long-term vision of the EU, but most preferred to spend their time on the problems immediately in front of them.

Leaders of smaller countries can sometimes be very effective strategists. When Lee Kuan Yew became the first prime minister of independent Singapore in 1965, he took over a small island which had just separated from its larger neighbour Malaysia, with few economic advantages beyond its position on the trade routes, and beset with racial tensions. He saw the opportunity to position Singapore as a base for high-tech industrial investment in the first wave of globalization. He therefore set a grand strategy combining economic openness and high standards of technical education with conservative social policy and tight political control. By the time I was serving in Singapore in the mid-1970s, the policy framework was already firmly in place, and the foreign investments which were to ensure the island state's prosperity were already flowing in. Lee maintained the same strategy throughout his thirty-one years in office and a further fourteen years as Senior Minister. The result was a spectacular record of economic growth and political stability. When some British politicians imagine post-Brexit Britain as 'Singapore-on-Thames', they overlook not just the vast differences of scale and geography between the two countries, but the decades of applying a consistent strategy that went into Lee Kuan Yew's success.

The Singapore of Lee Kuan Yew was not exactly a Western-style democracy: elections never yielded more than a handful of opposition parliamentarians and press coverage was deferential. But Lee did make a genuine effort to listen to public opinion and to explain what he was doing. Leaders further along the scale of authoritarian rule than Lee ever was can set out sweeping strategic plans without fear of being held to account by public or parliamentary opinion. They can as a result make disastrous mistakes, as the succession of Soviet five-year plans and Mao's Great Leap Forward followed by the Cultural Revolution showed. Since that time, the Chinese system has developed a real capacity to use long-term planning to produce sustained economic growth. President Deng Xiaoping's policy of modernization, which he termed 'Socialism with Chinese characteristics', was pursued pretty consistently for more than thirty years and turned China into an economic superpower. Xi Jinping has staked out a similarly long-term vision of turning domestic economic strength into political and military dominance in Asia by the 100th anniversary of the People's Republic in 2049.

Putin has also pursued an international strategy which has become clearer over the years since his arrival in power in 2000. In amongst all the tactical manoeuvrings, the central objectives seemed to be to right the wrongs done to Russia in the years after 1989, to restore the country as a force to be reckoned with, and to take advantage of America's retreat from international engagement in order to expand Russia's sphere of influence and stable of client states. In that, Putin was very successful. But he was far less so in domestic policy. He failed to modernize or diversify the economy, which remains heavily dependent on gas exports and is hampered by a range of Western sanctions. The result of Putin's approach since 2001 has been that Russia now faces a much more fundamental strategic choice, between seeking an accommodation with the West, to which it is connected by history and which provides its main markets, or becoming a junior partner to an increasingly dominant China.

Regimes that do not have vocal opposition or freedom of speech find it easier to set out grandiose visions and long-term plans. But since these are not tested and contested in democratic public debate, they can turn out to be flawed or lead to unforeseen consequences. Fisher Ames, a member of the first US Congress in the 1790s, spotted the difference between representative government and autocracies when he compared the latter to a merchant ship 'which sails well, but will sometimes strike a rock and go to the bottom', while a Republic (he could not yet say a democracy) 'is a raft, which would never sink, but then your feet are always in the water'.[18]

Britain's problem with strategic thinking

Britain's feet are certainly in the water. My starting point in accounting for the poor track record of British governments in recent decades in long-term strategic thinking is the nature of the British political system, and specifically the absence of a written constitution. This has long been regarded by British politicians as a great strength, allowing the system to adapt to changing circumstances without the rigidities of a written text. Observers of the British system from abroad often marvelled at how the political system seemed to function on the basis of unwritten conventions and gentlemen's agreements. They watched with admiration as elections produced stable majorities, and the losing party moved smoothly into the role of Her Majesty's Loyal Opposition. They also noticed that a British prime minister with a sizeable majority was in a very powerful position. In this they were right.

The corollary of an unwritten constitution is that the checks and balances on the government's actions are relatively weak. Parliament is sovereign, and an inconvenient law can be changed – so long as the majority holds. As a result, prime ministers spend a great deal of time nurturing their parliamentary majority, because their power stems from that. This is a further pressure on top of all the others pulling British prime ministers towards short-term decisions. It is especially acute when majorities are small, as has been the case in recent decades with the governments of Major, Cameron and May. But even large majorities can be fractious, as Johnson found out from the series of rebellions in the course of 2020.

In my experience, British prime ministers tend to operate in this environment by some combination of inner conviction and tactical manoeuvring. The mixture varies, but both are usually there, and neither favours strategic thinking. When Blair arrived in power in 1997, he had plenty of conviction, and a track record of outmanoeuvring opponents in the Labour Party in his rapid ascent to the top job. I was working on Bosnia and Kosovo in the FCO at the time and saw Blair in action from that vantage point. He was always a decisive leader with strong views. But after the 9/11 attacks he was a changed man, more driven, haunted by the risk of further and even more deadly attacks. He recounts in his memoirs that as soon as he heard about the attacks he was certain about what to do: 'It was war. It had to be fought and won. But it was a war unlike any other. . . it was a battle for and about the ideas and values that would shape the twenty-first century.'[19] In other words, an ideological battle, and a very Blair-shaped one in which he immediately saw himself playing a leading role. He threw himself into an exhausting round of globe-trotting in the weeks after 9/11, visiting European capitals, the US, the Middle East and Pakistan. The intensity of his conviction carried him into volunteering the UK as the first lead nation for the NATO operation in Afghanistan. And it was fundamental to his decision to follow George W. Bush into Iraq.

From what I saw of Blair in the run-up to Iraq (by this time I was Political Director in the FCO) he was still driven by his dark vision of the risk that Islamist terrorists could get their hands on nuclear, biological or chemical materials and use them to mount an even more devastating attack on the West. As he said to the Chilcot Inquiry into Iraq, 'The crucial thing after 9/11 was that the calculus of risk changed.'[20] It was for Blair an emotional calculus rather than one based on any evidence that Saddam Hussein might actually let terrorist groups get their hands on such dangerous materials. The fact that Saddam had for years been flouting obligations laid on him by the Security Council to open up to UN inspectors became in Blair's mind an unacceptable risk for the West. Britain would not in my judgement have gone to war in Iraq without the force of Blair's convictions. None of his senior ministers were as certain as he was, and some (Robin Cook, Clare Short) were clearly opposed. Such is the power of the prime minister's position when backed by a parliamentary majority that it was Blair's burning certainty rather than a shared process of strategic thinking about the balance of risks which led Britain into war.

It is equally true that there would not have been a British referendum in 2016 on the EU without the convictions of David Cameron. He resembled Blair as a politician in some ways. Both were thoughtful leaders who took their responsibilities very seriously. Both had risen seemingly effortlessly to the top job without prior ministerial experience; both were good at the day-to-day decision-making which dominates a prime minister's life.

The lack of effective checks and balances on a prime minister, coupled with a preference for conviction politics over strategic thinking, led each man to make one fundamental error for which they will always be remembered. For Blair, it was Iraq. For Cameron, it was his decision to call a referendum, unleashing forces which swept Britain to precisely the destination he wanted to avoid. In his memoirs, he pulled back the curtain on his thought process: 'How are the biggest decisions made? They are usually rooted in convictions and beliefs. They tend to be contemplated for a long time, but are often expedited by circumstances.'[21] Although Cameron had been thinking about a referendum for some time as a way of responding to the rising anti-European sentiment in his party, his decision was very much a personal one, and without the kind of strategic appraisal of the pros and cons which Macmillan commissioned in 1959. Indeed, Cameron followed Thatcher's 1989 example by banning civil servants from planning for the consequences of a failure of his policy. He used the power of his office to force it through despite the reluctance of his closest political ally, George Osborne. Kate Fall made a telling comment about Cameron's approach to governing in her book about the eleven years she spent as his Deputy Chief of Staff in opposition and government. Referring to how he wanted his new NSC to function, she commented: 'David doesn't want NSC to turn into a "talkathon", so he steers it away from endlessly discussing strategy. He fears such discussions will be too broad brush and easily ignored. Instead he favours specific problem-solving.'[22]

When he took his fateful decision, Cameron cannot have been fully aware of the depth of anger and alienation bubbling in the country beyond the major cities, or of the high risk that the referendum would ignite this explosive mixture of grievances. One of the puzzles of recent British political history is why the much-vaunted practice of MPs returning to their constituencies each Friday to take the pulse of the country appears to have failed to warn the Prime Minister of what he was walking into. It is one of the many parallels with what was happening at the same time in the US. The mainstream Democrat and Republican candidates in the 2016 election race were also caught short by Trump's ability to connect with a large block of voters with grievances they had largely overlooked.

Britain and America were two of the countries to feel the greatest force from the populist politics of identity and grievance. It is surely no coincidence that in the Reagan/Thatcher era, the same two countries had been the most enthusiastic exponents of deregulation. Later they went furthest in opening up their economies to globalization, and with their large financial sectors, they were among the hardest hit by the 2008 crash. The US lost 20 per cent of manufacturing jobs in the two decades after 2000, many of them after 2008. Real wages in Britain were stagnant for a decade from 2009. Both saw massive cuts in public services through the years of austerity. In both countries, the losers from globalization looked on as bankers continued to collect their bonuses.

In 2016, the Leave campaign in the UK and Trump in the US tapped into this deep well of anger much more effectively than the established political parties. They were both masters of the populist art of mobilizing their base of supporters with sound bites tailored to appeal to the bitterness of those who felt their identity threatened by change they had no control over. The slogans implied a return to an imagined golden age before job losses and immigration ('Make America Great Again', 'Take Back Control').

In the UK, May (who succeeded Cameron as prime minister in the summer of 2016) inherited from the referendum a mandate to leave the EU but no manifesto on what a future relationship between the UK and the EU should look like. The Leave campaign knew what it was against, but not what it was for. After the bitter divisions of the referendum campaign, May should have slowed the political pace, and called all the various factions from the campaign together to hammer out some degree of common approach to what kind of future relationship with the EU would best serve Britain's interests. As Sir Ivan Rogers, who was Britain's Permanent Representative to the EU until he resigned in 2017, put it:

> what we needed to do very early on was to recognise the complexity and inevitable longevity of the exit process, work out our viable options, achieve real clarity about where we wanted to land, having worked honestly through the very tough choices we faced – and still do face – and reconcile ourselves to a serious period of transition.[23]

It was a moment of profound disruption in the established pattern of Britain's international relations and it cried out for strategic thinking. May missed that opportunity. She had the power but no real convictions as to how to use it. She reverted to instinct and tribal politics. She gave priority to persuading the triumphant Brexiteers in her party that, although she had supported the Remain side, they could depend on her from now on to keep the faith. Within weeks of taking office and with minimal consultation with her Cabinet, she made a speech at the Conservative Party conference which put Britain on a trajectory to the hardest form of Brexit, including leaving the EU's single market and customs union and excluding any role for the European Court of Justice.

In March 2017, May pressed ahead using the powers of the office to invoke the two-year process for negotiating Britain's departure, still without having reached a consensus even within her own government on the nature of the future relationship. This led her into a downward spiral as she spent two years trying to reconcile the contradictions in her opening position and negotiate a deal which would be acceptable to the EU and to the increasingly restive Conservative Party in the House of Commons. Her plight was made worse by her impulsive decision to call a general election in the summer of 2017, which left her without an overall majority and dependent on the votes of the hard-line Democratic Unionist Party of Northern Ireland. Without a majority, all the powers of the prime minister's office ran through May's fingers like sand.

May tried to negotiate increasingly tortuous ways around the contradictions in her policy in conditions of great secrecy, and then to bounce them through the House of Commons. She failed repeatedly to secure a parliamentary majority and resigned in the summer of 2019. Johnson, chosen by the Conservative Party to succeed her, showed from the outset that he was determined first to get a majority in the Commons and therefore get the levers of power working again, and second to get Britain out of the EU in short order. He fought another ruthlessly effective campaign and secured himself one of the largest post-war majorities. He then did a hasty renegotiation of parts of the Withdrawal Agreement with the EU which he inherited from the May government, and pushed it through Parliament with minimum debate.

Johnson is also an instinctive politician. But his instincts led him in a very different direction from May's on the future relationship between the UK and the EU. Johnson set out an objective which was purely political: to assert an untrammelled British sovereignty, and specifically to secure the right to diverge from EU rules and regulations. The Trade and Cooperation Agreement (TCA) finalized at the end of 2020 reflected these choices. The EU was much more focused on protecting its economic interests and competitive advantage. As a result, the TCA allowed trade in goods (in which the EU enjoyed a large surplus with the UK) to continue without tariffs or quotas, while the services industry (where the UK was a major global force) faced far higher barriers. Johnson had in practice chosen a rhetorical sovereignty over the country's economic interests. Rhetorical, since no British government was likely to take advantage of their sovereign right to slash environmental or food standards, or working conditions. And if they did so, the EU had taken care to write into the Agreement the option to reimpose tariffs.

Negotiating a trade agreement with a much stronger economic power always involves painful concessions. A strategic approach would have involved making a detailed economic impact assessment of the decision to give such priority to sovereignty over a closer economic relationship with the EU. When Covid-19 struck, there was another strategic opportunity to pause the negotiations with the EU and assess the combined impact on the British economy of the pandemic and a hard Brexit. But that option was not taken. The policy remained unchanged. As a result, on top of the devastating effects of the pandemic, the economy faced an additional reduction of 5.2 per cent of GDP over fifteen years, according to Britain's Office for Budget Responsibility.[24]

Johnson and his team continued to use in the business of running the country the blunt instruments of populist campaigning. The Prime Minister's criteria for choosing his senior ministerial colleagues seemed to be personal loyalty and enthusiasm for Brexit. His advisers came from the ranks of the Leave campaign. Then the Covid-19 crisis struck. Overnight, competence and strategic thinking became far more important than campaigning prowess. And the government was found badly wanting, as measured both by the economic impact and the numbers of excess deaths in the course of 2020. It would be unfair to blame this all on ministers confronted with an unprecedented catastrophe. All governments faced massive challenges. The pandemic also showed up with brutal clarity structural weaknesses in Britain's National Health Service which was underfunded and overly complex, and an overburdened elderly care sector which had been neglected for decades. Public Health England was too slow to realize that its centralized testing system was incapable of scaling up fast as the pandemic spread. In a detailed account in *Atlantic* magazine, the journalist Tom McTague concluded that Britain was 'a country that believed it was stronger than it was, and that paid the price for failures that have built up for years'.[25]

These underlying problems were however compounded by a style of political leadership which treated the response to Covid-19 as yet another campaign to be won. There was the initial bravado, as the virus spread on the continent, that Britain was exceptional, protected by its renowned scientific and medical sector. The government failed to think ahead and organize sufficient supplies of Personal Protective Equipment (PPE) for NHS staff and the care home sector, which was largely left to fend for itself in the early months, with disastrous results. Decisions on successive lockdowns were left too late. There was a constant tendency to over-promise and under-deliver.

As a campaigning technique, setting an eye-catching target (such as that Brexit would produce £350 million a week for the NHS) was effective, even if the figure was inaccurate. But in a public health crisis, over-optimistic claims chip away at public confidence in the government's competence. New targets for the PPE to be distributed or the number of tests to be carried out became a regular feature of government briefings. But they never seemed to be met, despite continuing claims of Britain's 'world-beating' performance. Britain, like other countries, struggled to create a workable system of testing and tracing those with the virus and their contacts. But after every setback, Johnson deployed the technique of the ever-more-ambitious target. In most cases, these targets were not met. The exception was Britain's very successful vaccination campaign launched in late 2020. Here, clear decisions taken early in the pandemic to invest massively in vaccine development and supply enabled the government for once to achieve an ambitious goal.

In a symbol of their approach to governing, the Prime Minister's closest advisers moved during the Covid-19 crisis in the summer of 2020 into a so-called Command Centre, apparently modelled on the control room at NASA made famous from the moon landings. They reportedly sat in front of screens showing real-time data relayed from government departments. Although the innovation did not outlast the departure of the Prime Minister's Chief of Staff, Dominic Cummings, in late 2020, it seemed to sum up the Johnson government's fixation on day-to-day crisis management. Gordon Brown and his close team set up a similar nerve centre surrounded by TV screens in the frenetic closing period of his prime ministership in 2009–10. They called it the horseshoe. When the team around a political leader get so obsessed with the immediate that they treat governing a country as if it was running the trading floor of a bank, all hope of longer-term strategic thinking has gone.

The handling of Britain's departure from the EU and of the Covid-19 crisis points to some conclusions about why British governments struggle with strategic thinking. They have been pushed like all democratic governments towards short-termist crisis management by the pressures of the media and social media. On top of that, British politics has been poisoned and polarized by the populist appeal to grievances and nostalgia rather than rational, fact-based policymaking. Disillusion with governing elites (as a result of failures like Iraq and the inequalities generated by austerity) has fuelled distrust of experts and independent advice. Personal loyalty has come to matter more than competence in the allocation of top jobs. The powers of the British prime minister with a pliant majority, unfettered by a written constitution, were often used for a process which Cummings called 'creative destruction'. Throughout that period, there was more evidence of destruction than creation.

The failures of strategy and governance in the years after the Brexit referendum have done lasting damage to Britain's economy, and exposed serious weaknesses in the political system, which had seemed on the surface to be so stable and resilient. Britain is in urgent need of reviving the art of strategy, which was such a feature of the post-war years. In making the hard choices which lie ahead, it will also be vital to muster all the powers of influence the country still possesses.

6

FINDING THE POWER TO INFLUENCE

What can Britain do about the changing global geometry?

*Yes, this does break international law,
in a very limited and specific way.*
Brandon Lewis, Northern Ireland Secretary,
House of Commons, 2020[1]

Britain's double jeopardy

The end of the era of US internationalism would have been tough for Britain even if the country had still been in the EU. It now faces the double jeopardy of adjusting to this new geometry of global power while defining a new set of national priorities outside the EU. To have any chance of lasting, this recalibration needs to be based on a realistic assessment of the country's interests and the damage to its international reputation as a result of the chaotic departure from the EU and the mishandling of the Covid-19 pandemic.

Every British government has its own formulation of the country's national interests. The National Security Strategy of 2015 grouped them neatly into three objectives:

- To protect our people at home, in our Overseas Territories and abroad, and to protect territory, economic security, infrastructure and way of life.

- To protect our global influence – reducing the likelihood of threats materialising and affecting the UK, our interests and those of our allies and partners.

- To promote our prosperity – seizing opportunities, working innovatively and supporting UK industry.[2]

However formulated, this is the bedrock of what citizens expect their governments to deliver. The first, protecting the country's people and way of life, is the primary duty of all governments. It is at the heart of national security policy and has been one of the main themes of this book. But the nature of the task is changing fundamentally with natural hazards now thrust to the top of the agenda.

The second objective on projecting global influence invites the question of whether Britain really is still a country with global interests or whether this assumption is out of date. Britain's sense of itself is deeply bound up with its glorious past as a major world power. The seafaring exploits of the first Elizabethan age are one of the few parts of British history still taught in schools. The country's imperial past has left its legacy in an instinctively international outlook[3] and the Commonwealth, the worldwide network of fifty-four countries sharing ties of history, language, values and administrative and judicial traditions.

The Commonwealth's value as a multilateral organization can easily be overstated – it will never become a load-bearing political organization as some nostalgists hope. None of the other leading countries of the Commonwealth see it as any longer central to their interests in the world. But family and cultural ties are immensely strong. The arrival of millions of people in Britain from Commonwealth countries in the decades since decolonization means, for example, that tensions on the Indian subcontinent are immediately felt in communities across Britain. Imperial history also accounts for the numbers of British expatriates abroad, far more widely spread than any other European country. Although there is no systematic collection of data, one survey suggests that over 5.6 million British people were resident abroad in 2010, with communities over 1,000 strong in more than 100 countries.[4]

The world has come to Britain as a result of the country's past, so it has no option but to stay engaged in the world and maintain its influence. As the Cambridge historian of international relations David Reynolds commented in his recent book *Island Stories*:

> . . .we need to move beyond the idea of a self-contained 'island', portrayed as adopting various roles over the centuries – empire, Europe, the globe – as if these could be tried on and then taken off, like a suit of clothes. In reality, 'we' have been made by the empire, Europe and the world as much as the other way round.[5]

Britain's global past is still very present in the structure of the economy. The country's stock of overseas investments was worth £11 trillion in 2017, almost twice the size of that of France, an economy of comparable size. The value of foreign investment in the British economy was even higher at £13 trillion.[6] Britain was at the forefront of the first wave of globalization, benefiting through its open economy and Thatcher-era deregulation to win a significant share of foreign investment in global supply chains. British companies were among the pioneers in setting up manufacturing units to benefit from lower wage costs in developing countries. With its strong financial centre and well-developed high-tech start-up community, Britain's services sector is genuinely global in its reach.[7]

Imperial history has also left Britain with a worldwide network of military bases, some of strategic importance when it comes to global influence, such as the airfields on Cyprus, Diego Garcia (leased to the US) and Ascension Island, and naval facilities in Bahrain and Singapore. The total of sixteen bases is still the largest of any country except the US. Among European countries only France has anything like this geographical span. Britain's armed forces are still designed to be deployable anywhere in the world. The entry into service with the Royal Navy of two large aircraft carriers equipped with the latest-generation combat aircraft in 2020 and 2023 respectively ensures that this will remain the case for decades to come, even though the UK will in practice only be able to deploy them with supporting vessels from other allies.

The British brand is still attractive in the world. The Portland Soft Power 30 index[8] has published rankings since 2015 based on measuring objective data and international polling for a wide range of countries. The index has consistently ranked Britain at or near the top, scoring highly for culture and education, reflecting the global impact of British sport, films, music, and the appeal of its universities, museums and tourist sites. It also ranked highly for engagement, that is, its diplomatic network, development programme and openness to the world, and for its digital infrastructure and high-tech sector. In 2019, the UK fell from first to second place, behind France, having been first in 2018. Not surprisingly, it lost ground over the soap opera of Brexit and the effect on business confidence as demonstrated by falling foreign direct investment. And that was before the global downturn which followed the pandemic.

Factoring all these variables into a new strategy for Britain is made more difficult by the very different strands that made up the majority for leaving the EU in the 2016 referendum. In amongst these, there were two quite distinct approaches to Britain's international role. The London-based leaders of the Leave campaign such as Johnson set out an expansive vision of unleashing Britain's potential, liberating it from the shackles of the EU and 'taking back control' in order to resume its traditional place as a global power at the heart of the Anglosphere. For this group, a large part of the attraction in leaving the EU was the escape from European regulations, from workers' rights to environmental norms. Some saw Britain as a super-competitive Singapore-on-Thames. However, many of the supporters of the Leave campaign outside the metropolitan areas saw very different advantages in leaving the EU. For them, taking back control meant counteracting the effects of globalization and limiting immigration. It implied a protectionist stance towards a world seen as threatening to the traditional British (or more accurately English) way of life.

One thing Leave supporters seemed to agree about was the country's greatness and exceptionalism. A Deltapoll among a sample of British adults in late 2019, for example, showed that 36 per cent of respondents who had voted Leave ranked Britain as the most important country in the world, and an overall majority put Britain second behind the US.[9] But they had contradictory views on what that meant in practice. These underlying contradictions make it all the more difficult to plot a way out of Britain's double jeopardy. And it is just as unhelpful to good policymaking to overrate Britain's weight in the world as it is to get trapped in a gloomy foreboding of inevitable decline.

The country's destiny surely lies between the two. What powers of influence can the country really muster to give it the best chance of making a success of its new post-Brexit career?

The power of example

Britain was widely respected around the world as the pioneer of individual rights and freedoms. Although Magna Carta was written in 1215, some of its declarations still jump off the page in this era of nationalist strongmen:

> No free man shall be seized or imprisoned or stripped of his rights, or possessions, or outlawed or exiled, or deprived of his standing in any other way, nor will we proceed with force against him, or send others to do so, except by the lawful judgement of his equals or by the law of the land.[10]

The ancient procedure of habeas corpus, where a judge has the power to demand the presence in court of someone who claims they have been locked up unlawfully, was another early British judicial innovation, as was the idea of a constitutional monarchy with the sovereign subject to laws made in Parliament. Britain can justly claim credit for developing the rule of law, and its legal system still has a global reputation. It is one of the key underpinnings of the success of London as a financial centre. This also has downsides. Those with doubtful fortunes to hide have long found London a convenient place to stash their ill-gotten gains, although the introduction of Unexplained Wealth Orders is starting to make life more uncomfortable for them. Dissidents from many countries have been attracted to the UK by its legal protections. But they have sometimes been pursued by assassins from their own countries, as the poisoning of the Skripals in 2018 and the unexplained murder of other Russian citizens have shown.

For all that, the British achievement in evolving a system of constitutional monarchy and parliamentary sovereignty (without violence since the seventeenth-century civil war) gave the Mother of Parliaments a worldwide renown. The union of England, Wales, Scotland and Northern Ireland in the United Kingdom has survived with modifications since 1707, and the devolution of power to regional assemblies in all except England has been an example of pragmatism and adaptability in constitutional arrangements. The success of the British and Irish governments in negotiating an end to the thirty-year-long IRA terrorism campaign in Northern Ireland and across the UK set an example of conflict resolution and reconciliation between divided communities. The 1998 Good Friday Agreement put both governments in a strong position to offer help and support to others facing civil war and ethnic division.

Britain's reputation as a bulwark of the rule of law and one of the founders of the post-war order also gave it a certain moral authority in holding other nations to account when they failed to live up to the same standards. The UK often played a leading role in the UN Security Council in pressing for sanctions against countries which violated international law, for example by invading neighbours (Iraq over Kuwait in 1990, Russia over Crimea and Ukraine in 2014), pursuing illegal nuclear or chemical weapons programmes (Iraq, Iran, Libya, North Korea) or violating human rights (in the Balkans, Rwanda and Liberia). Most recently, the British Mission to the UN was responsible for drafting the resolutions imposing an arms embargo on the warring factions in the Yemen.

The fact that Britain was seen by many nations as a leading light in upholding the rule of law added to the shock when Blair sided with the Americans in 2003 over the invasion of Iraq without a clear Security Council mandate. Opinion polls in the US suggest that Blair's backing helped shore up support for George W. Bush's policy. The counterfactual question is also interesting: would the US have been able to go ahead if Blair had pulled Britain out in the final weeks? In military terms, the answer is clearly yes, but it could well have resulted in a faster and steeper decline in public support for the war in the US. In the much less dramatic circumstances of the proposed US/UK/France attack on Syrian chemical weapons sites, the British Parliament's decision to deny Cameron a mandate led Obama, as we have seen, to push the decision to Congress, and thereby to kill the operation.

I have used the past tense so far in referring to Britain's reputation as a champion of parliamentary democracy and the rule of law. These have been a core part of the country's power of influence in the world. But they have been damaged by the polarizing effect of Brexit on British politics. The conventions safeguarding the functioning of Parliament and the independence of the judiciary have come under particular strain. One of the Johnson government's early acts when they arrived in power in the summer of 2019 was to prorogue (that is, suspend) Parliament for the unprecedented period of five weeks at a crucial point in preparations for Britain's departure from the EU, which was at that time scheduled for 31 October 2019. It took a judgment by the Supreme Court to overturn what was widely seen as an attempt to avoid parliamentary scrutiny.

Following the general election in December 2019, and on the strength of a majority of eighty in the House of Commons, the government then made a sustained effort to reduce Parliament's role in the whole Brexit process by greatly expanding the use of so-called Henry VIII powers. These are clauses in legislation which give powers to ministers to make subsequent changes to (or repeal) parts of a law with minimal, or in some cases no, parliamentary oversight. The pretext for their widespread use in Brexit legislation was the need to have flexibility to make regulations given the uncertainties over the outcome of negotiations with the EU on the future relationship. But the effect was to shift power in a significant way from the legislature to the executive.

The Covid-19 emergency prompted the government to go further still in this direction, by taking sweeping emergency powers under the Coronavirus Act 2020 – powers that would normally only be accorded in wartime. They enabled ministers in effect to rule by decree, imposing heavy restrictions on individual liberties (such as rules on the numbers of people who could gather together, or curfews and other restrictions on business), often published only hours before they entered into force and with no prior parliamentary debate. In some cases, the House of Commons were only able to consider regulations of this kind months after they had entered into force. This massive extension of executive power eventually led enough Conservative MPs to threaten a rebellion in September 2020. The government were obliged to concede that measures imposing restrictions across the whole of the UK would be subject to a vote in Parliament. Nonetheless, they continued to exercise far-reaching powers to make regulations applying to large regions of the country.

The degree of uncertainty surrounding the UK's future relationship with the EU in the summer of 2020, and the need for a rapid public health response to curb the spread of Covid-19, both gave some grounds for delegating time-limited powers to ministers. But these Henry VIII clauses are habit-forming. They make it all too easy for a government with a large majority to force through laws while minimizing troublesome parliamentary scrutiny over their implementation. The effect is to erode the sovereignty of Parliament and strengthen the hand of the executive.

This trend has been further reinforced by the Johnson government's moves to curb the role of judges in checking the legality of its actions through the process of judicial review. The Supreme Court ruling on the prorogation of Parliament evidently annoyed the government, and led to a pledge in the Conservative manifesto in the 2019 election to ensure that judicial review was not 'abused to conduct politics by another means or to create needless delays'. The government asked a panel of carefully selected lawyers in 2020 to make recommendations on legislation. But ministers made no secret of the trend of their thinking. The Home Office published a video in August 2020 complaining of 'activist lawyers' delaying and disrupting efforts to return migrants, and the Prime Minister referred in his party conference speech the following month to the criminal justice system being 'hamstrung by lefty human rights lawyers'.[11]

All these trends came together in the Internal Market Bill introduced into Parliament in September 2020. Its original purpose was to divide up the regulatory powers which Brussels returned to the UK as part of the Brexit settlement between Westminster and the devolved administrations in Edinburgh, Cardiff and Belfast. The bill was festooned with Henry VIII clauses. It also included wording intended to exclude the courts from any scrutiny of the way in which ministers used their sweeping powers. The House of Lords Constitution Committee in a scathing report described this as putting 'ministerial regulation-making powers above the law in an unprecedented manner. It would be an unacceptable breach of the rule of law.'

The Internal Market Bill gained particular notoriety because it also contained the clauses to which the Northern Ireland Secretary Brandon Lewis was referring when he made the extraordinary statement quoted at the head of this chapter about a willingness to break international law. The government had got themselves into a mess on how to preserve an open border between the north and south of Ireland once Britain had left the EU single market. The two sides were agreed from the outset on the principle that whatever the future trading arrangements between them would be, these should not disturb the great legacy of the Good Friday Agreement which the open border represented. The EU demanded some means of ensuring that this open border did not become an unsupervised back door for smugglers and fraudsters in and out of their single market. The May government spent two years searching for an option that would keep the Irish border open and also avoid the need for a customs border in the only other place possible: down the Irish Sea, separating Northern Ireland from the rest of the UK for customs purposes. She failed to find one which was acceptable to her party. When Johnson became prime minister, he accepted (in the Northern Ireland Protocol to the Withdrawal Agreement he signed with the EU in late 2019) that there would indeed be a customs border between Northern Ireland and the rest of the UK, but publicly declared that Northern Ireland businesses would have 'unfettered access' to Great Britain, in direct contradiction to the terms of the Protocol. In the end, the rhetoric of sovereignty could not obscure the fact that the Protocol imposed a whole new system of checks and bureaucracy on thousands of traders and hauliers. The government were caught between the international agreement they had signed, and the very different commitments they had made publicly.

In an attempt to extricate themselves, the government of the country which invented the rule of law were reduced to threatening openly to break international law. At the last moment, the UK and EU found a pragmatic solution to the problem of overlapping jurisdictions in Northern Ireland in the Trade and Cooperation Agreement agreed with the EU at the end of 2020, and the government let the offending clauses drop. They may have been intended mainly to pressure the EU into making concessions in the final stages of the negotiations. But the very fact of making the threat to walk away from a treaty obligation damaged Britain's credibility in holding other countries to account when they breach international agreements. It overlooked Britain's vital national interest as a global trading power outside the main economic blocs in striking free trade agreements with a wide range of countries, all of whom needed to trust London to uphold legal commitments, even when they become politically inconvenient. Taken together with the other measures to erode parliamentary sovereignty and the independence of the judiciary, this episode undermined Britain's claim to be a beacon for the rule of law and a country which sticks to its word.

There is no prospect of Britain's political parties agreeing to produce a written constitution. The only alternative, in response to the bonfire of the unwritten conventions of British political life, would be to put more of them into laws, in order to prevent worse abuses in the future. Honesty and integrity are a vital building block of democracy, and they became a casualty of the bitter partisan divisions which have torn such a gaping hole in the fabric of British politics. The damage to the country's power of example is likely to be lasting.

The power of ideas

One of the messages of this book is that the success of the post-war order was based not just on American dominance but on the power of ideas to shape the international landscape. Britain has always been good at drafting treaties and setting norms. As we have seen, British ministers and their advisers came up with some of the key concepts behind the United Nations and NATO. In the international financial area, John Maynard Keynes was a central player in the negotiation of the International Monetary Fund and World Bank. Britain was the leading force in the creation of the Council of Europe and the Brussels Treaty on Western European Union, both in 1948.

Once Britain joined the EEC, it championed ideas which changed the organization in fundamental ways. The Single Market, one of the defining achievements of the European project, was only agreed in the 1980s because it was driven through by Thatcher and her European Commissioner Lord Cockfield. After the fall of the Berlin Wall, Britain was the leading voice in calling for the enlargement of what was by then the EU to embrace the former members of the Warsaw Pact. The combination of these ideas left the EU a very different organization. It was double the size with, at its heart, a genuinely common market free of all regulatory barriers.

Britain's success, in bending the EU in the direction of a liberal trading system and playing a leading role in stabilizing Eastern Europe, increased London's value to Washington as an ally. In return, British ministers and their diplomats were often very effective in coming up with workable solutions to problems the US and UK were both facing when the US inter-agency process was bogged down in internecine warfare.

Britain has had a strong track record in extending the reach of international law. We saw in Chapter 1 how – in the view of some scholars – human rights law grew from a seed planted by Churchill in the Atlantic Charter. It certainly developed with significant British input through the Universal Declaration of Human Rights in 1948, the European Convention on Human Rights in 1950 and the International Covenant on Civil and Political Rights in 1966. The same applies to the doctrine that individuals could be held to account by an international tribunal for war crimes. British jurists worked with their American counterparts on the Nuremberg tribunal at the end of the Second World War. This precedent was followed by the war crimes tribunals for the Balkans and Rwanda in the 1990s. By the time of drafting the Rome Statute of 1998 setting up the International Criminal Court, Britain had taken over the leading role from the Americans, since the US refused to become a party, unwilling to see its armed forces personnel subject to the jurisdiction of a foreign court. International agreements, particularly the UN Convention Against Torture adopted in 1985, also extend the personal responsibility of public officials.

Predating all these are the Laws of War, starting with the first Geneva Convention in 1864, which set out to provide 'the basis on which rest the rules of international law for the protection of the victims of armed conflict'. The series of four Geneva Conventions and a range of Protocols which developed over the following 150 years established three key principles to guide the decisions of commanders: the distinction between civilians and combatants, proportionality in the use of force, and the avoidance of unnecessary suffering. British lawyers contributed extensively to the development of this body of law regulating the conduct of war, which set widely accepted standards for the humane treatment of civilians, prisoners of war and wounded military personnel. As the US and British governments found during the occupation of Iraq, even isolated breaches of these standards by small groups of soldiers cause serious reputational damage.

The Laws of War thus retain a moral force. But they need to adapt as military technologies and tactics change. Targeted killings using drones controlled by an operator many thousands of miles away have implications for the distinction between combatants engaged in the heat of battle and non-combatants. The speed of the latest missiles will mean that defensive systems have to react without any human intervention. With advances in artificial intelligence, it will soon be impossible to reconstruct the criteria which a weapon uses to select and strike a target. With its long experience in overseeing the Laws of War, the International Committee of the Red Cross has already begun work on this. Britain is well qualified to give an international lead in this area.

The regulation of the digital world is another issue where there is real urgency. Domestic laws have already been changed in Britain and many countries to cover cyber crime. Stealing commercial secrets by hacking into computers is a crime in the same way as stealing folders of documents from a filing cabinet. Swapping pictures of child abuse is no less a crime for its being conducted through internet chat rooms. But there is no international code of conduct, or anything equivalent to the notion of mutual deterrence which developed around nuclear weapons.

The first step towards international regulation of the most dangerous consequences of cyber attack came in the UN Secretary-General's Group of Experts in 2013, which included Russian and Chinese representatives. Their report[12] found that the provisions of the UN Charter applied to actions in cyberspace. A second report in 2015[13] confirmed that 'State sovereignty and the international norms and principles that flow from sovereignty apply to the control by States of Information and Communications Technologies activities' carried out in their territories. That would mean, for example, that large-scale media manipulation would breach the principle of non-interference in internal affairs, and an attack on a nuclear power station or air defence networks could reach the threshold triggering the right of self-defence. Cyberspace is not, therefore, a lawless environment beyond the reach of international law. But it is a wide gulf between declaring those abstract principles and agreeing an international code of conduct setting limits in the interests of all internet users. This is the sort of practical legal problem which British experts helped clarify in drawing up the Geneva Conventions and framing arms control agreements. The UK has a clear national interest as an advanced digital economy in helping to establish some rules of the road in cyberspace. As societies become ever more dependent on internet connectivity, British ideas and drafting skills could help strengthen the rule of law in a vital area for the future.

There are many other areas where the long British experience in generating solutions to problems which can bring countries together, and then turning them into international agreements, will be needed in the years ahead. Two of the most pressing are expanding the common ground among states on carbon reduction measures, and strengthening the global regime protecting public health. Taking a leadership role on issues such as these is another reason for re-establishing respect for the rule of law as an essential pillar of British foreign policy.

The power to persuade

Having ideas is only a part of the answer to exercising effective influence. Imposing them needs leadership, an effective international network and sustained hard work. The vision of the Atlantic Charter only got translated into the institutions of the post-war world by years of work to get the UN, NATO and the rest off the ground. In the British parliamentary system, strong political leadership means having a stable majority in the House of Commons. Britain's first-past-the-post electoral system has traditionally delivered a clear result. This helped leaders like Thatcher and Blair have greater international impact. Winning a strong mandate at home gives a new political leader credibility with his foreign counterparts. They are also more likely to do deals if they are confident that these will stick. The period of near-hung parliaments between 2010 and 2019 was a real handicap for Britain's power to persuade.

In Cameron's premiership, his foreign counterparts could never be sure if he could deliver at home. The loss of the parliamentary vote in 2013 on Syrian chemical weapons exacerbated those fears, which were fully borne out by the 2016 referendum result. May's inability to get the House of Commons to back the successive deals laboriously agreed with Brussels weakened further an already threadbare negotiating hand. The fact that throughout this period ministers often had to loiter in London waiting for the next cliff-edged vote meant that they could not be working the international networks of influence. Long trips to places such as Asia or South America became almost impossible for much of the year. Britain was largely absent from the international scene for the three years after the referendum. Johnson's commanding majority from the 2019 election should have created the opportunity to rebuild Britain's influence in international affairs, but at the time of writing there is no sign of a change in the self-absorbed and inward-looking nature of British politics.

British ministers enjoy reeling off the list of all the international clubs the country belongs to and to point out that, even after Brexit, this is more than any other country. A typical list would include Britain's permanent membership of the UN Security Council, and its seat at the tables in NATO, the Commonwealth, the G7 and G20, the Organization for Security and Co-operation in Europe, the Organisation for Economic Co-operation and Development, the World Trade Organization, the International Monetary Fund and the World Bank. These give a shape to Britain's international engagement. But international influence does not come just from having a seat at as many tables as possible. It has to be earned by the willingness to take initiatives and then pursue them by building coalitions of interest and support. Ministerial time and energy are essential for this. So is effective staff work. British diplomats in international organizations have long been rated highly by foreign counterparts for their professionalism. They make a real contribution to the country's soft power. In the UN Security Council for example, UK representatives will often hold the pen in drafting resolutions, trusted by other members to craft a compromise text which will be minimally acceptable to all (the fact that English is normally the working language of international negotiation works in their favour). The combination of a British minister at the table, using debating skills honed in the House of Commons, and talented staff in support who can work the room and shape the final outcome, can prove highly effective.

Britain's network of embassies and consulates is one of the largest in the world, with 274 in total spread across 169 countries.[14] But in practice these are often very small operations, with only a handful of career diplomats and no real capacity to lobby and persuade at the top level. For decades the FCO, lacking a forceful domestic lobby to argue their case, lost out in the Whitehall resource battles and their budget declined as development spending, the intelligence services and the armed forces were given priority. The number of career diplomats fell from around eight thousand at the end of the Cold War to little more than half that in 2015, though they are finally starting to rise again after Jeremy Hunt announced in 2018 the target of recruiting 1,000 new staff in two years (both career diplomats and staff hired locally by embassies on fixed-term contracts).[15]

In June 2020, the Prime Minister announced the merger of the FCO and the Department for International Development (DFID) in order to 'unite our aid with our diplomacy and bring them together in our international effort. . . . in a new Department charged with using all the tools of British influence to seize the opportunities ahead'.[16] DFID's budget in 2019 was just under £11 billion, while the FCO's was less than £3 billion. I can imagine that eyes lit up in British embassies around the world that the years of famine were over, and that the new department would have the resources to pursue British interests without the scrimping and saving which had become so much a part of life for the Cinderella department of the UK's international effort. If the FCDO (Foreign, Commonwealth and Development Office), as the new department is called, becomes the powerhouse of a coherent international policy preserving the best of both previous departments, that will be a real benefit for post-Brexit Britain. It will only happen if it is a genuine merger, not a takeover by a cash-hungry Foreign Office intent on using the development budget as a 'giant cashpoint in the sky', in the unfortunate phrase Johnson used in the House of Commons when announcing the decision.

Over its twenty-three years of existence, the DFID built a worldwide reputation as a leader in development policy. In 2005, Blair's government committed to meeting the UN target of spending 0.7 per cent of GDP on development assistance. That target was finally met under Cameron's government in 2013, making Britain one of a handful of developed countries to do so. That was a major national asset, not just in relations with countries that received aid, but much more widely as a demonstration that the country was serious about promoting its values by tackling global poverty, disease and malnutrition.

In late 2020, the government decided to make a massive reduction in development spending to 0.5 per cent of GDP in 2021–2, explaining this as a short-term response to the pressures on public finances as a result of the pandemic. But choosing to abandon the 0.7 per cent target sent a much wider message about the government's international priorities: Britain could afford to step up spending sharply on military equipment, but it would be cutting programmes for the world's poorest with very little notice, in the middle of the pandemic. There was no coherence between the two decisions. The development programme was not only a major soft-power asset enhancing Britain's power to persuade, but a hard-headed contribution to international stability, thereby reducing the likelihood of military interventions, which are far more expensive. It will be important for the new FCDO to get the best possible development value from the reduced budget.

The power to act

Throughout my career, British diplomats envied the capacity of the French foreign ministry to come up with an initiative in order to resolve a current problem or damp down a conflict. We joked that the keyboards in the French foreign ministry had a special key which would add a sentence at the end of any ministerial statement to the effect that France would shortly be calling a conference of all the interested parties in Paris. The French system seemed to find it easier to launch the bare outlines of the proposal and leave it to others to flesh it out and help it fly, or to shoot it down. French ministers always seemed willing to accept the risk that an initiative might not get off the ground, or that it might fail to deliver useful results.

When I was Ambassador in France, the then foreign minister, Laurent Fabius, ploughed huge efforts into trying to breathe life into Israel–Palestine peace efforts after the US Secretary of State John Kerry gave up in despair in 2014. He called a series of short-notice conferences in Paris, to which a British minister would reluctantly come, often on a Saturday morning. The attempt got nowhere, but did Fabius's reputation no harm. There seemed to be a willingness in the press and the National Assembly to accept that it was part of France's natural role to be at the forefront of new thinking, and that the risk of failure was a price worth paying.

Macron showed another aspect of French diplomacy when he threw out, in the course of a speech in 2017 about the future of Europe, the idea of a European Security Council. It was an intriguing concept, but there was absolutely no detail, except the hint that it would be outside the EU and so potentially a vehicle for Britain to stay engaged with its European neighbours on foreign policy. There was no further detail, either at the time or in the three following years. The idea lay on the table, with a large French flag on it. Any attempt to be more precise (for example on membership) would have led to loud protests from any country left out. Was the idea that there would be permanent and non-permanent members? What powers might the body have and how would it relate to the EU and the UN? Silence from Paris. If the concept took off, France would get the credit. If it was a damp squib, Macron would at least have been seen in France as a thought leader, even if others were too unimaginative to follow his lead.

British ministers would in my experience have been much more risk-averse, wanting reassurance that all the details of an idea had been worked out before putting a proposal on the table, and needing to be convinced that it would not fall flat on its face. They would have worried about a grilling in the House of Commons and criticism in the press. In carving a niche for Britain outside the EU, post-Brexit governments would do well to take a leaf from the book of the entrepreneurial French if they are to get their ideas into circulation.

Being the first to grasp the initiative is far from the only measure of successful diplomacy. But it is not much good having powerful ideas and broad networks of persuasion if the incentives on ministers are all to avoid risk and play safe. If Britain is to re-establish an influential role in international affairs, ministers will have to be ready to take risks and show agility in spotting opportunities to influence the course of events. The government has long experience of organizing high-level international gatherings. Convening and chairing an international conference gives the host nation real opportunities to shape the outcome if skilfully exploited.

Typically, the host drafts the concluding document. There are limits to how far the host can tilt the text in their favour, since they need to get the agreement of all the others, or at least to ensure no one blocks it. But the benefit of drafting the text and running the meeting already gives the home team an advantage over most others. The power of holding the pen can be considerable. British diplomats are adept at distilling an agreed text out of a rambling discussion or, if all else fails, producing a 'Chairman's summary'. That does not commit other delegations but becomes the conclusion of the meeting and dominates the closing press conference. Hosting a successful international meeting can enhance a country's reputation. The British are good at it, but it requires ministers to put time and effort in advance into building coalitions of success and narrowing down the areas of difference.

Achieving a more direct impact on events will be much more difficult outside the EU. The use of sanctions is an example. As we have seen, Britain has been one of the most active countries in pressing for sanctions against countries which breach their international law obligations or abuse human rights. On the strength of a reputation for scrupulously upholding international law, and a respected intelligence community capable of producing credible information about wrongdoing, British diplomats were often at the forefront of action in the UN to impose sanctions. With the Security Council largely deadlocked in recent years, Britain switched its efforts to promoting EU sanctions, particularly against Russia over its invasion of Ukraine. Outside the EU, the British government has a new capacity to act independently and to move quickly on sanctions policy. It used that new agility in imposing, together with Canada, sanctions on Belarus in October 2020, at a time when the EU was held up by disagreements among members. But independence of action comes at the price of effectiveness. Unless the EU or the US or both are prepared to follow, UK sanctions are unlikely to have much impact.

How much influence can Britain realistically expect to have on the changing geometry of global power? The answer will depend partly on how the tension is resolved between the internationalism which is Britain's inheritance and the narrower nationalism which was one of the main themes of the Vote Leave campaign. It will also need fearless advice from the government's professional advisers in the Civil Service.

Since the Northcote–Trevelyan reforms of 1855, the British public service has been politically neutral, with promotions and appointments made on the basis of merit, not the political favour of ministers. In their first eighteen months, the Johnson government challenged that convention in two ways. First, a number of political appointments were made to jobs which had previously been filled by civil servants. The clearest case was that of former FCO diplomat David (now Lord) Frost. After leaving the Civil Service, he served Boris Johnson when Foreign Secretary in a political role as a Special Adviser. When Johnson became prime minister, Frost became, in 2019, Europe Adviser, conducting the negotiations with the EU, although a plan to make him also National Security Adviser was later scrapped. The effect was to blur the distinction between the neutral role of the civil servant and the political advice of a personal ally of the Prime Minister. The second aspect was a much more adversarial relationship between the political advisers around the Prime Minister, particularly his Chief of Staff Cummings, and senior civil servants. This led to the ousting of Permanent Secretaries (the top civil servant in a government department) at an unprecedented rate, with five leaving in six months during 2020. In some cases, they were made to carry the can for a failed policy. In other cases, the sudden departure of the top official seemed to follow clashes with the minister or an impression that Permanent Secretaries were resisting change. The appointment of a former Treasury official, Dan Rosenfeld, as the Prime Minister's new Chief of Staff in early 2021 promised a more constructive relationship between the political and civil service sides of Whitehall. That is essential given the scale of the challenges the country faces. Public servants need to feel that they can give ministers honest advice and unwelcome news without fear of losing their jobs in order for the government to make sound policy decisions and use Britain's powers of influence effectively.

———

Britain's reputation for competence and reliability has been tarnished in the eyes of many international observers in the years since the 2016 Brexit referendum. How deep and lasting the damage proves to be will depend significantly on whether the bitter divisions over Europe reduce over time. Britain still has real strengths as an international power, even though the political and public estimate of its power to influence is higher than the reality. But the British system has a deep-seated problem in standing back from the constant succession of crises in order to rediscover the art of strategy. Like other Western countries, it has also found it difficult to choose and stick to a few key priorities in its security policy. Ensuring some British influence in the changing shape of global power will be a continuous balancing act for British governments. Its political leaders will need the ideas and the force of persuasion to offer practical solutions to some of the many problems crowding in on the world's democracies.

PART III

Making Hard Choices

7

TRIANGLE OF TENSION: BRITAIN, AMERICA AND CHINA

Dare to struggle and be good at fighting.
Xi Jinping, September 2019[1]

*I am a Sinophile and I believe we must work
with this great and rising power.*
Boris Johnson, June 2020[2]

*I'll. . . mobilize a true international effort to
pressure, isolate and punish China.*
Joe Biden, October 2020[3]

When I created the role of National Security Adviser in 2010, I wanted to use it to help fill the gap in the upper reaches of Whitehall on strategy-making. So I brought together a group of the Permanent Secretaries of all the government departments represented on the NSC. I knew, because I had been one of their number, that this was a frustrated group. They had spent their careers becoming experts in their various fields. But when they had reached the top, they rarely got their hands on the big policy issues, because they spent so much time running their complex organizations and fighting for resources. They were an untapped reserve of talent that could be deployed to do the wide-ranging thinking that was so often missing.

My group of officials met in advance of every meeting of the NSC, to prepare the discussions of our political masters. But we also escaped every couple of months for an early evening three-hour strategy discussion over a glass of warm white wine in a room at Admiralty House in Whitehall, which boasted a few rather uncomfortable chintz sofas. The best discussion we ever had was in 2011 on the issue of China. It brought together two completely different Whitehall communities working on China, who rarely met in any other forum. In one camp were the economic evangelists, who saw China as a massive and growing source of trade and investment for a British economy staggering after the 2008 financial crash. Their public spokesman was the Chancellor, George Osborne, who predicted in 2010 a golden decade in UK–China relations. In the other camp were the securocrats, who saw China developing fast into a major military power, increasingly assertive in its neighbourhood, forcing Western investors to share the intellectual property in their technologies and conducting cyber attacks to steal any information that might give them an industrial advantage. Both views were right then. They still are, but it has become much more difficult for Britain to reconcile them as US–China tensions mount.

The transition from one international order to another has often involved conflict between a ruling power and a rising challenger. The historian Graham Allison coined the term 'Thucydides trap' in his book exploring the likelihood of conflict between America and China, *Destined for War*.[4] The ancient Greek historian had famously outlined his trap in his *History of the Peloponnesian War*: 'It was the rise of Athens and the fear that this instilled in Sparta that made war inevitable.'

Allison did not argue that war between America and China was inevitable. He and his Harvard students developed a Thucydides Trap Case File of sixteen occasions over the last five hundred years when a rising power challenged a dominant one. They found at least four where this had happened peacefully. It is relevant that two of their four cases happened since the invention of nuclear weapons. One of them, Russia's challenge to the US in the Cold War, came very close indeed to a nuclear conflict at the time of the Cuban Missile Crisis in 1962. The other – Germany's challenge to the position of Britain and France for political influence in Europe in the 1990s – seems to me to be a very marginal case for inclusion in this list of confrontations between great powers. A third case study was the replacement of Britain by the US as the dominant global economic and naval power in the late nineteenth and early twentieth century. That is a much better example of the conditions in which one international order can make way peacefully for another. The American historian and former senior administration official Kori Schake studied this transition in her book *Safe Passage* and summed up:

> Looking across a hundred years of America growing stronger and more assertive in the international order, the most striking element is how highly contingent a peaceful outcome was in the transition from British to American hegemony. This peacefulness hinged on a unique sense of the political sameness, both domestically and in international practice, for the crucial years of America surpassing Britain that allowed the hegemon to diminish the importance of relative power between them.[5]

That sameness of political culture and international outlook is very obviously missing from the Chinese challenge to American dominance. Schake concluded that the ideological differences between China and America meant that, if there were to be a hegemonic transition (that is, a complete replacement of one dominant power by another), it would require imposition by force. Allison thought that the outcome of the China–US confrontation would depend on the leadership in both countries. They would need to find a way for China with its 1.4 billion people to resume the prominent position it enjoyed for much of human history without the sort of hegemonic transition which would lead to war.

The world Britain will be seeking to influence in the coming decades will be shaped mainly by this US–China confrontation. It has often been referred to as a new Cold War. But superficial analogies can mislead. There are vast differences between the forty years of East–West conflict and what is happening between the US and China. Unlike the Soviet Union in the Cold War, China is an economic and technological superpower, and is forecast to become the world's largest economy on any measure by the mid-2020s.[6] China and the US start from a position of deep economic integration. They are each other's largest trading partner, whereas the Soviet Union was always a minor player in world trade. Washington and Moscow were engaged in an ideological competition to impose their political and economic system on the world. China does not seem to have any ambitions to do that. Indeed, Beijing contests the very idea of a universal set of values and norms of behaviour. Their favourite part of the UN Charter is the keep-your-hands-off provision in Article 2:

> Nothing contained in the present Charter shall authorize the United Nations to intervene in matters which are essentially within the domestic jurisdiction of any state or shall require the Members to submit such matters to settlement under the present Charter.[7]

The Cold War was overshadowed by the military confrontation between East and West, with the nuclear arsenals of both sides on hair-trigger alert. There is a significant military dimension to the US–China stand-off. The Chinese defence budget is the largest in the world after the US, bigger than those of the UK, France and Germany combined, and growing at over 6 per cent a year. Many of the new weapons they are deploying, such as long-range anti-ship missiles, seem intended to push the US Navy out of the South China Sea while China continues to militarize the area. As the US, British and other allied navies step up their patrolling in these waters to assert their right of freedom of navigation on the high seas, localized conflict by miscalculation or accident is a constant risk. In addition, Taiwan has long been a potential flashpoint, given the US commitment to defend the island against a Chinese invasion. But China is not seeking global military competition with the US, and is far too smart to take the sort of risks which led to the Cuban Missile Crisis. The US–China confrontation will not be played out primarily as a military struggle but a competition for technological and scientific supremacy. That in itself is a seismic change in the geometry of global power.

China's integration into the global system in the two decades after Deng Xiaoping's opening up of the Chinese economy in the 1980s was a turning point in the world economy. When it became clear that Deng Xiaoping's China would develop into an economic superpower, it was evidently in the West's interest to enmesh it, for example by inviting it into the World Trade Organization in 1991. There was a strong element of political calculation in this as well. There was plenty of evidence of the repressive nature of the Chinese Communist Party even under the modernizer Deng Xiaoping.

I was part of the negotiations with the Chinese government in 1982–4 on the future of Hong Kong. These led to the 1984 Joint Declaration, in which China pledged to preserve Hong Kong's way of life for fifty years. Britain had neglected to move towards representative government in Hong Kong up to that point, and Deng Xiaoping rejected out of hand any form of democratic development in Hong Kong after 1997. The killings in Tiananmen Square in 1989 showed how brutal the regime could be. Nonetheless, many Western China-watchers hoped that growing prosperity in China, the emergence of a large middle class and the experience of hundreds of thousands of Chinese students at Western universities would all, over time, fuel pressures within China for more personal freedom and ultimately more of a say in how China was governed. The internet seemed to increase the prospect that Chinese people would be able to get a glimpse of Western lifestyles and freedoms and want the same for themselves.

Those hopes have been dashed. But they were not unreasonable at the time. The two Chinese leaders who succeeded Deng Xiaoping, Jiang Zemin (president from 1993 to 2003) and Hu Jintao (2003–13) were cautious and pragmatic men, whose priority was China's economic development, and who were willing to cooperate with the West to achieve this. Western investment in China boomed. The relocation of manufacturing to the highly efficient factories of China, and the optimization of global supply chains which went with it, was one of the key engines of global growth, lifting billions out of poverty. China largely respected its obligations in international agreements such as the WTO. In the same way, it mostly stuck to the commitments it made in the Joint Declaration, particularly in the economic area, although there was growing Beijing interference in the governance of

Hong Kong. Economic cooperation seemed to be in everyone's interests, and was the best way of ensuring that the rise of China would happen within an adapted system, avoiding the risks of the Thucydides trap.

That trend towards closer engagement between China and the West, under way since the 1980s, has now been decisively reversed. The central question, which has far-reaching implications for British foreign policy, is how far the decoupling will go and how much of the global trading system can be preserved in an age of profound mistrust between its two most important players. The main reason for this reversal comes down to one man: Xi Jinping, who became Party Leader in 2012 and President in 2013. With China launched irrevocably on the path to becoming an economic giant, he turned his energies on strengthening the Party's grip on every aspect of China's economy and society. His intolerance of dissent was soon evident in the purges in the Party and state structures. Repression of the Uighur community in Xinjiang was stepped up. When a protest movement broke out in Hong Kong in 2018 against a change to the law which would have made extradition to mainland China easier, the authorities first tried heavy-handed policing tactics, and then in 2020 imposed a draconian national security law, effectively demolishing the personal liberties which China had pledged in the Joint Declaration to maintain.

An early sign of the fracturing in the facade of globalization came in the area of the internet. Soon after he came to power, Xi confounded Western hopes about the beneficial effects of Chinese citizens' access to the World Wide Web by erecting a digital firewall to prevent access to Western material. Behind this barrier, the Chinese authorities harnessed the latest technology to develop an internet of state control, where access to foreign information is censored and the state could monitor where an individual is, their health and the nature of their online browsing. These Orwellian tools of state surveillance were tried out first in the repression of the Uighurs. They have since been applied throughout China. It was this network of control which enabled the Chinese authorities to enforce restrictions on movement during the pandemic and probably helped them bring it under control rapidly.

The dream that an open, unrestricted internet would be a tool for bringing countries and peoples together is dead. The decoupling has already happened between the American-based capitalist internet, dominated by massive corporations like Google, Facebook and Amazon who generate huge profits from mining the data of users for advertising, and the state-controlled Chinese internet. The EU still hopes to promote a third way on regulating the internet based on high levels of individual privacy and data protection. But, as in many other areas, Europe will struggle to sustain a separate model in a world of great power competition.

Xi Jinping's ambitions were not limited to total control in the domestic realm. He also embarked on a much more assertive foreign policy. The Belt and Road infrastructure initiative was designed to ensure that China dominated Asia–Europe trade flows. The militarization of the South China Sea threw down the gauntlet in terms of his ambition to replace the US as the indispensable power in Asia.

Trump's priority when he arrived in the White House was US–China trade. One of the principal planks of his election campaign had been to bring back factory jobs to America by using the tariff weapon to cut China's massive surplus in manufactured goods. That policy failed: the US trade deficit in goods with

China, which was $347 billion when he arrived in power, was still $345 billion three years later.[8] It had been a very unusual sort of trade war. After four years, the American appetite for Chinese manufactured goods was undiminished, and Chinese consumers still bought far more Apple iPhones than any other brand, over seven million of them in the second quarter of 2020 alone.[9] But others in the Trump administration had a more radical agenda than simply waging a tariff war: they sought to block China's technological ambitions and end American dependence on China for high-tech equipment. This campaign gathered pace after China adopted in 2017 an intelligence law providing that 'any organisation or citizen shall support, assist and cooperate with state intelligence work.'

As a result, all Chinese-owned technology firms operating in the US came under suspicion that they might be passing Americans' personal data back to the Chinese government. The concerns crystallized around TikTok (a video-sharing app owned by the Chinese technology firm ByteDance and downloaded 100 million times in America). The fact that a Chinese-owned tech company was handling the data of so many Americans drew the attention of the powerful US Committee on Foreign Investments. Their ruling in the summer of 2020 that Chinese ownership of TikTok's American business was against the country's national security interests opened the way for Trump to force ByteDance into a restructuring, which in effect separated off the US business and put it under close US official supervision.

Tensions which had been brewing between the US and China for years all seemed to come to a head in the first half of 2020. China's evasive initial response to the outbreak of Covid-19 and the aggressive 'wolf warrior' diplomatic campaign they mounted to deflect the blame, coincided with the Hong Kong crackdown, a flare-up of tension on the Sino-Indian border and the intensifying US pressure on Chinese tech firms. And the US administration chose this moment to step up their tech war with China with a concerted bid to drive the Chinese telecoms giant Huawei out of the US market and to kill its bid to be a leading global supplier of 5G technology. This is where the UK found itself trapped in the force field of US–China confrontation. The episode sheds much light on the dilemmas Britain will face in an era of mistrust and rivalry.

Britain's security services knew a lot about Huawei products, probably more than any Western intelligence organization. Since 2010, GCHQ had been running the Huawei Cyber Security Evaluation Centre in a nondescript business park at Banbury in Oxfordshire. This laboratory was paid for by Huawei and allowed GCHQ engineers to take apart randomly selected pieces of Huawei's 3G and 4G equipment and search for any sign of bugs or malicious code before they were plugged into the UK telecoms system. We know from the annual reports published by the National Cyber Security Centre,[10] that they were worried about the quality control on the products they dismantled and studied. But they never found any evidence that the Chinese firm had built in back doors to allow data to be stolen by them or the Chinese authorities.

When it came to whether the UK's telecoms operators like BT could install Huawei kit in their new 5G networks, the NCSC advice was that the characteristics of 5G made it important to keep Huawei equipment out of the most sensitive bits of the system where data was encrypted for transmission and decrypted at the other end. But they judged that the risks were manageable if Huawei equipment was confined to the edges of the networks, such as the antennae which would be needed in far greater numbers to obtain countrywide 5G coverage. The only other suppliers of 5G equipment at that time were two European companies, Ericsson and Nokia. Their equipment was more expensive and less advanced. The NCSC experts saw value in the operators using equipment from all three suppliers to increase resilience of the network.

British decisions also had to take account of growing US hostility to Huawei. This began with concern at Huawei's aggressive pursuit of market share around the world, including what the US considered to be a major breach of the sanctions against Iran. It led to the high-profile arrest of a senior Huawei executive, Meng Wanzhou, in late 2018 on a visit to Canada on the basis of a US arrest warrant. But as the wider US–China confrontation intensified, the administration focused hard on the risk of Chinese intelligence-gathering. US pressure succeeded in keeping Huawei out of the Australian market and those of several other allies. They were lobbying the British government to take the same approach.

Britain's NSC nonetheless agreed in April 2019 that Huawei should be allowed to supply equipment for the non-core parts of Britain's system. We know that because someone promptly went and briefed the *Daily Telegraph* on the details of the discussion. This was the first serious leak from the British NSC in its nine years of history. The Defence Secretary Gavin Williamson lost his job over it, though he denied being responsible. The Americans moved fast to capitalize on the opening the leak had given them. The tone of their briefings to the British press can be judged from the *Daily Telegraph* headline a few days later: 'Huawei deal like giving Beijing a "loaded gun": US warns against letting Chinese firm help build 5G network as May faces backlash'.

The leak turned the issue into the first test case of how Britain outside the EU would position itself in the US–China struggle for dominance. The Huawei decision was delayed. Over the following months, it became even more political. Johnson, in campaigning to succeed May, in the summer of 2019 pledged to deliver 'full-fibre broadband to every home in the land' by 2025 – much earlier than the previous goal of 2033. The only possible way of achieving that was to skip the stage of fibre-optic cables altogether and move fast on the roll-out of wireless 5G coverage. Trump had meanwhile pulled the Huawei issue into the centre of the China–US trade dispute with an Executive Order in May 2019 banning US firms from using information and communications technology from any company considered a national security risk.

The NSC prepared to take another run at the Huawei decision in January 2020 with Boris Johnson in the chair. At that point, the decibel level from Washington increased dramatically. A delegation led by US Deputy National Security Advisor Matt Pottinger descended on London shortly before the meeting to present what they claimed to be new information and to warn ministers that using Huawei technology in the UK would put transatlantic intelligence sharing at risk and would be 'nothing short of madness'.[11] In case the Brits failed to get the message, a member of the delegation warned menacingly that 'Donald Trump is watching.' Another recent member of the US national security staff turned up on British airwaves suggesting that a Huawei deal could put a free trade agreement with the US in jeopardy. Back in Washington, Republican Senator Tom Cotton was preparing a bill linking intelligence sharing with the UK to use of Huawei equipment.

To their credit, the NSC stood their ground, trusted their experts and essentially confirmed the decision initially taken by May. This was elaborately wrapped for US consumption, with a cap of 35 per cent on participation by any one telecoms provider in the UK 5G network in the interests of encouraging competition and diversity of supply. Within six months, the decision had unravelled. This period coincided with the sharply deteriorating relations between China and the West The mood amongst Conservative MPs turned decisively against China. China's security crackdown in Hong Kong intensified. The British government responded robustly, offering the prospect of permanent residence in the UK to some three million Hong Kong people entitled to a British passport. Ministers may have hoped that the worsening political row with China could be kept separate from decisions on future telecoms infrastructure.

What made that impossible was a further intervention from Washington. A further round of US sanctions in the summer of 2020 made it illegal for any manufacturer to sell microchips (a key component of all telecoms products from smartphones to the most sophisticated equipment) to Huawei which were developed or produced using US technology. The measure exploited the fact that China had no indigenous supplier of advanced chips, which came mainly from Taiwan. It amounted to a lethal blow against Huawei's business in much of the world. One effect was that British experts could no longer be sure that future Huawei equipment would be made from reliable components. The NSC therefore met again in July 2020, and decided this time that Britain's telecoms operators would be barred from buying new Huawei 5G equipment from the end of 2020, and that all the company's kit remaining in the UK's 5G network should be removed by 2027. They did not go as far as some hardliners had been demanding: that Huawei products, even in the 3G and 4G networks, should be removed in short order, which would have meant roads being dug up across Britain and probably blackouts in the telecoms network. The NSC decision was presented as a technical response to changes in market conditions, and ministers acknowledged that it would delay the roll-out of 5G by two to three years and cost at least £2–3 billion. The hard reality was that Britain had bowed to American industrial coercion.

The central US objection to Britain giving Huawei a role in its 5G market was not that it imposed an immediate risk to national security. The detailed papers released by the NCSC showed how carefully the technical risks of allowing a limited Huawei role had been examined and discussed with US experts. Britain's intelligence heads would never have recommended a course of action to ministers which posed a serious threat to the crucial intelligence sharing relationship with the US and other allies. The purpose was to ensure that Britain was on the American side of the growing high-tech war with China. And the glaring weakness at the heart of the American case was that they did not have an alternative home-grown technology of their own to offer. They were therefore left urging Britain to use equipment from Ericsson and Nokia, both of which made extensive use of Chinese components.

The noisy American opposition to Huawei masked a remarkable failure of strategic foresight. If all parts of a 5G network were of such overriding national security concern that the US was willing to call into question intelligence cooperation with the UK, why on earth had the US not developed their own 5G solution? That was a question which influential American voices, including Senator Newt Gingrich, threw back at the US administration after the initial failure to keep Huawei products out of the UK market.

The pressure on Britain over Huawei came not just from the Trump administration and the Republicans in Congress. The

Democrat leadership on the Hill were also strongly critical of the British decision. The whole US political system was waking up to the fact that the US and its allies had inadvertently allowed themselves to become dependent on China's manufacturing powerhouse. The result was that China had become the world's leading producer, not just of consumer products like mobile phones but technologies of strategic importance for the future, from telecoms to artificial intelligence and large batteries. Correcting that will be a long process. Changes in the software world can be applied rapidly, as the TikTok case showed. But decoupling supply chains, building new factories and training workers in Western countries to replace the high-tech manufacturing capacity in China will take years.

The decision-making in London on Huawei in 2019–20 showed that, for all the claims made for Brexit in terms of taking back control, ministers were unable to make a decision on the balance of Britain's interests allowing a limited role for Huawei. They were obliged by US sanctions legislation to accept a policy of banning Huawei equipment which British experts did not believe was necessary. Inevitably, when the US pushed matters as far as they did on Huawei, the British government had no choice but to go along with them, whatever the cost. But the whole episode was a reminder that in relation to China, British and US interests will not always be the same.

Britain will never be equidistant between the US and China. London's vital defence and security relationship with Washington and the stake both countries have in the other's economy will ensure that London's relationship with Washington will always be on a completely different level from that with Beijing. However, the US as a superpower can better afford an adversarial approach to China.

The pendulum has swung a long way in Western capitals in a few short years since political leaders were championing China as the economic partner of choice. China's own actions have badly damaged its reputation, from its human rights abuses including the use of forced labour, its theft of intellectual property and refusal of reciprocal market access. Yet many democratic countries have balanced a much tougher political approach to Beijing by striking economic agreements. In the course of 2020, China concluded a 'first phase' trade deal with the US, a Regional Comprehensive Economic Partnership with fifteen Asia-Pacific countries including Australia, Japan and South Korea, and an investment agreement with the EU.

Britain is not part of any of these agreements. But it also has a pressing need to maintain a functioning commercial relationship with the vast and growing Chinese market, given that the British economy lost over 10 per cent of GDP in 2020,[12] the sharpest fall of any major industrialized country, at the same time as the country embarked on a more distant relationship with its main trading partner, the EU. Britain also has a greater need than the US for a working system of rules governing trade and economic relations, given that its smaller economy is heavily dependent on international trade. The more US–China rivalry deepens, the more important it will be for Britain to preserve the capacity to work with both sides, including on issues of global governance such as climate change, public health and rules of trade and investment. Britain has the experience to play a leading part in shaping a new relationship between China and the West, recognizing that they are at the same time strategic rivals and economic partners.

An unsettling feature of the Huawei episode was that the US administration was willing to threaten even its intelligence relationship with the UK in a ruthless show of power politics – and that the British government were willing to call their bluff. That was a reminder of how relative the special relationship has become, at least for Washington. It was truly special when the two countries were close allies in the Second World War. Even then, Britain was the junior partner, and relations became increasingly lopsided as the US contribution in terms of manpower and military supplies dwarfed Britain's.

The special relationship cliché lingers on in British political parlance, the outward and visible sign of the unspoken strategic assumption that Britain should strive to be America's closest partner. I often thought that senior Americans cultivated a particular smile for use when British ministers made it too obvious how important it was to them to have the assurance of hearing the phrase repeated. It was not a smile of scorn. US interlocutors readily accepted that in some of the most secret areas of national security the partnership with Britain was irreplaceable. It was a smile of recognition that this incantation was essential for British self-confidence, but also a slightly embarrassing reminder of how unequal the relationship had become.

The intelligence relationship is unique. Britain is the only ally that can begin to match America's global reach. GCHQ and its American counterpart, the National Security Agency, have a unique degree of mutual dependence. The capacity of Britain's JIC to produce concise intelligence assessments of complex issues at speed has long been valued in Washington. This is something the American system, with its multiple agencies hawking competing assessments, all clamouring for the attention of political leaders, has struggled to do.

The nuclear weapons cooperation between the UK and America is also genuinely unique. The US has been willing to share successive submarine-launched intercontinental ballistic missile systems, first Polaris then Trident, for the British nuclear deterrent, at a fraction of the cost of developing separate systems. This is the most visible part of the long and deep tradition of defence cooperation dating back to the Second World War. The two armed forces continue to be closely intertwined: Britain has been alongside the US in all its main expeditionary wars since Vietnam, and sends much of its officer corps to the US on staff college courses.

All this cooperation is deeply rooted, mutually beneficial and, up to a point, insulated from the political weather. In return for their decades of subsidising the British national security effort, the Americans got a loyal ally who mostly shared their world view, interpreted that world through the filter of the same intelligence and, when it came to fighting, did so with the same doctrines and mostly the same kit as American units. The Biden administration will no longer use the intelligence relationship as political leverage on the British government. But with bipartisan backing from Congress, they will expect allies to support them in their challenge to Chinese dominance of high-tech manufacturing and its blatant stealing of Western technology.

As US priorities shift to great power competition and to Asia, the degree of overlap between British and American international priorities will inevitably reduce. Leaving the EU both increases the relative importance to Britain of its relationship with Washington and weakens its value further to the US, which valued Britain's presence at the EU decision-making table. Despite British defence budget increases, there is bound to be a lingering doubt in the US national security community as to whether the British could really be relied on to be with them in a crisis if that required sending forces into combat. The 2013 British parliamentary vote against the use of force in Syria and the growing gap between US and British military capabilities both create uncertainties which did not exist before.

British governments will have to make difficult decisions as they navigate the force field between Washington and Beijing. One of these is to accept that Britain's national interest is not identical to America's in relation to China. Britain cannot afford to line up with the US in confrontation with China across the board. But if the choice goes against solidarity with Washington too often, the insulation surrounding the vital US–UK defence and security relationship could begin to come loose. Britain will face a continuing series of hard choices as it walks the tightrope between Washington and Beijing.

8

THE INTERNATIONAL SYSTEM
AND THE LURE OF THE NEW

The UK should use its convening power and thought leadership
to bring together nimble networks of like-minded nations. . .
House of Commons Foreign Affairs Committee, 2020[1]

One of the dilemmas facing Britain is choosing between the rhetoric of exceptionalism and the reality that the only way for a country of its size to have any real influence in the world is by making common cause with others. Those who campaigned for Britain to leave the EU were eloquent about the benefits of 'taking back control' but ambiguous if not evasive about what that meant for the country's role in the world. May's government never got beyond the slogan 'global Britain', with its echoes of the country's heroic past. This phrase appeared again in the speech Johnson made from the steps of Number 10 as he became prime minister in July 2019. He added a characteristic dash of British exceptionalism when he declared his mission to be:

> To recover our natural and historic role as an enterprising, outward-looking and truly global Britain, generous in temper and engaged with the world. No one in the last few centuries has succeeded in betting against the pluck and nerve and ambition of this country.[2]

The British government finds itself advocating 'global Britain' just as globalization is in retreat and the world is fracturing into spheres of influence dominated by the US and China. It seeks to bolster the country's international role just as the economy is staggering under the weight of the pandemic. In the course of 2020, ministers also resurrected another old cliché, that Britain should be a 'force for good' in the world. (I remember the MOD choosing this as their strapline when all government departments were required to have one in the Gordon Brown period. My favourite entry in the competition for an FCO equivalent was 'All over the place for you', although it didn't get chosen!) A notion of British exceptionalism was at the heart of the Brexit debates. It resurfaced regularly in Johnson's rhetoric as prime minister, not least in the frequent claims that Britain's response to Covid-19 was 'world-beating' when it was anything but. It could be heard in suggestions that it was time to move on from the old international order. Yet, to paraphrase Mark Twain when he read his obituary in the press, reports that the multilateral system is dead are greatly exaggerated. True, the pandemic and the rise of international disorder have shown up plenty of weaknesses. New groups of countries and new ways of working will be needed. But seventy-five years' worth of experience are not to be thrown away lightly. The British talent for institution building needs to be directed towards overhauling the existing machinery, as well as cutting a dash with ideas for nimble new networks.

Reforming the UN

Trying to reform the UN is an uphill struggle. The organization is sprawling, inefficient and often infuriating. The Security Council is logjammed by deep disagreements among the permanent members. Its legitimacy is weakened by the near impossibility of adapting its membership to shifts in economic and political power. Britain and France are the two permanent members whose positions look increasingly anomalous, at a time when countries like India and Japan have to seek election for two-yearly stints as non-permanent members. But neither Britain nor France is going to put real political energy into the campaign to enlarge the Council, let alone give up their permanent membership. The likelihood is that the Security Council will be increasingly sidelined as arm-wrestling between individual countries plays out just as it did during the Cold War. But at least, thanks to Alec Cadogan's ingenuity in 1945, members of the Council can use Article 27 of the Charter to haul up even the most powerful countries and hold their actions up to public scrutiny without being blocked by the veto. That may well turn out to be the Council's most powerful lever in the years ahead, and it is worth having.

In the years after 9/11, the UN set new global norms for counter-terrorism work and provided the clearing house where nations able to provide training and support were matched with countries with low levels of preparedness. The UN launched the global negotiation on climate change known as the Conference of Parties with the 1992 Framework Convention on Climate Change. That has developed into a remarkable exercise in multidimensional global negotiation open to non-governmental organizations and representatives of cities and business. It has allowed mounting public concern at the environmental damage being caused by carbon emissions to feed directly into the negotiations between governments. China's position changed significantly when public protests grew at the risk to health from air and water pollution. Even when Trump pulled the US government out of an active role, many US states, cities and businesses took the initiative to continue reducing US carbon emissions. Biden's decision to put the US back at the heart of the negotiations gives them a new impetus. But it is the UN which gives them globality and legitimacy.

The UN offers another advantage in the era of global threats to the survival of humanity. This is the network of specialized agencies. Some of these go back to well before the creation of the UN. The International Telecommunication Union is the world's oldest international organization, dating from 1865, but it now has a crucial role in setting new rules for the global internet. The International Labour Organization was founded just after the First World War. They have become UN agencies alongside a network established in the years after 1945 – bodies like the Food and Agriculture Organization, the UN Development Programme, the children's fund UNICEF, and the World Health Organization. They do vital work, largely out of the limelight, in tackling poverty, disease, malnutrition and setting global standards. They form a constellation of expert bodies spanning most of the most pressing issues facing the planet.

Covid-19 put the WHO in the spotlight and highlighted the weaknesses as well as the potential strengths of the UN Agency model. It started life with the noblest of ambitions. When the US joined in 1948, Truman declared that it would 'help liberate men everywhere from the overhanging cloud of preventable disease'. It has a track record to be proud of, for example, leading the successful effort to eradicate smallpox, which was achieved in 1979. It also has serious weaknesses. For example, it does not have the powers to insist on access to a country in order to investigate an outbreak of disease, unlike the International Atomic Energy Agency, which has such powers in the case of nuclear materials.

The WHO has a reputation for being risk-averse. The President of the UK's Royal Society, Venki Ramakrishnan, observed: 'My impression is that the WHO treats its scientific advice like some sort of academic research project. They wait for definitive evidence to emerge before they issue guidance.'[3] This caution reflects the problems of governance which have grown with the size of the UN. The WHO has an unwieldy governing board, made up of thirty-four people, and any of the 194 member states are entitled to speak at it. This is not a recipe for agile crisis response. Member state contributions only make up around half of its operating budget, with the rest coming from donations from foundations and other donors. It has received massive extra funding as a result of the pandemic, but this is short term and does not give it a stable platform to plan for the future. The US has been the largest contributor to the annual WHO budget; Trump's decision during the pandemic in 2020 to pull the US out could therefore have been disastrous for the organization. Biden overturned that decision and averted the immediate threat. But Covid-19 laid bare weaknesses in the governance and funding of the WHO.

Responding to those weaknesses is an urgent test case of whether the UN Agency system is capable of reform. The WHO has vital work to do as the only global public health body. If it cannot rise to the challenge of improved global cooperation on health even after the devastating shock of the Covid-19 pandemic, what hope is there that any other organization could be created with wide enough support around the world to do any better? And if a campaign to reform and strengthen the WHO gained momentum and widespread public support, the lessons could be applied to the way other agencies function as well, improving the world's capacity to spot new risks in many fields and act more effectively than the WHO and national authorities did in the early stages of the pandemic. Britain has a strong track record in medical science and research, demonstrated by the rapid development of the Oxford University/AstraZeneca vaccine against Covid-19. Despite the recent cuts in the development programme, this is still large, and widely respected for the distinguished contribution it has made over two decades to improving healthcare in the poorest countries. The British government is therefore well placed to play a leading role with the Biden administration and other interested countries to give the WHO new powers, improved governance and more stable funding.

Relaunching NATO

Can NATO also be adapted to the new geometry of global power? Is it worth a serious effort to renew the deal between the European allies and the US at the heart of the alliance? That matters to Britain because NATO is now the country's main international security anchorage. The scale of the challenge facing the organization was best expressed by an exasperated Macron when he called NATO 'brain-dead' in an interview with *The Economist* in November 2019. He timed this provocation to confront NATO leaders when they assembled shortly afterwards at a meeting outside London to celebrate the Alliance's seventieth birthday, the suggestion being that the organization no longer had a shared strategic purpose.

Macron was still furious about a sequence of events which had played out in the previous weeks. Trump had suddenly withdrawn US forces from Northern Syria, where they had been supporting Kurdish militia in their operations against ISIL. As soon as the US forces withdrew, President Erdogan sent Turkish forces across the border into Syria to attack the very Kurdish units the US had been supporting. Neither country gave any forewarning to

NATO allies, even though France was still working with the Kurds and had military personnel in the area – some of whom allegedly came under fire during the Turkish advance. What, asked Macron, did this lack of political consultations mean for the credibility of NATO's Article 5 collective defence guarantee? What if the Assad regime responded with a military offensive against Turkey – would other allies be willing to go to war in support of Turkey?

The question was prescient. In February 2020, Syrian forces with Russian support mounted air strikes against the Turkish forces in Syria, killing over thirty Turkish troops. Turkey promptly demanded formal consultations in NATO (potentially a step before invoking Article 5). Ambassadors of NATO countries duly assembled, offered their condolences for the death of Turkish soldiers, condemned the Syrian air strikes and expressed solidarity with Turkey. Appearances were saved, but the bigger question remained: if Syrian forces had crossed into Turkish territory, in retaliation for a Turkish intervention conducted without consultation with NATO allies, how many of those allies would have been willing to commit troops to a war with Syria?

NATO continues to be central to Britain's defence, as it has been since 1949. If anything, it has become even more important after Brexit as the only forum where British governments work continuously with friends and allies on the most important threats to their security. Given this dependence, Britain has a stronger incentive than any other member to lead in rebuilding the confidence between member states on which the whole NATO construct rests, and restoring at least some degree of strategic coherence to the organization. It would mean using up political capital on both sides of the Atlantic. But this would be a good investment, since the alternative of NATO gradually falling into irrelevance would leave Britain even more isolated in a dangerous world.

A NATO renewal campaign would need to appeal to the self-interest of all members. The Europeans and Canadians would need to be persuaded that sticking to their undertakings to continue increasing their defence spending, even with the pandemic pressures, was vital for maintaining long-term US engagement in NATO. European defence spending has been on a rising trend since the Russian invasion of Ukraine in 2014, but even so only ten out of thirty member states were meeting the agreed target of 2 per cent of GDP in 2020. Russia and China continue to spend heavily on their armed forces. After the Johnson government gave a big boost to defence spending in late 2020, London is well placed to urge others to make good on their announced increases and to target their spending on filling gaps in capability. Unless America's allies in NATO can show they are taking on more of the burden – even if slowly – no US administration will commit wholeheartedly to renewing the organization.

There is a second area where greater clarity from European countries is essential. That is what role the EU should play in defence. Although the EU institutions are wholly unsuitable to oversee large-scale military operations, President Macron has promoted the idea of 'European strategic autonomy'. This has its roots in French discomfort with NATO as a US-dominated organization. It expresses a long-standing French aspiration that, one day, the European project will be completed by the EU taking responsibility for its own defence. As concerns grew over Chinese dominance of high-tech manufacturing, Macron expanded his concept to cover greater European control of its own strategic industries and technologies. Germany has traditionally taken a more Atlanticist approach, seeking to strengthen the European role within NATO. But in the face of Trump's disparaging of NATO, Merkel moved in the direction of the French, calling in 2017 for Europe to 'take its fate into its own hands'.[4] Even though US–German relations are back on an even keel, the effect has been to push France and Germany closer together on defence, even though Berlin sees autonomy more in terms of efficient European defence industries than military separation from the US.

Strategic autonomy has always been an ambiguous, not to say slippery, term: autonomy from what precisely and for what purpose? The French concept of Europe becoming self-sufficient in defence without an American contribution is a fantasy in anything other than the very long term. Much larger and faster increases in European defence spending, particularly in Germany, would be needed even to begin to make up for the loss of American capability. One German analyst observed that in the area of intelligence alone, without US capabilities European states would be 'blind, mute and deaf. If they were attacked, they would have to defend themselves in a largely uncoordinated way, and face heavy losses.'[5] The very fact of talking, as Macron sometimes does, of a European army could encourage some in Washington to conclude that they no longer needed to invest in European security through NATO, even though the European countries are patently unprepared to counterbalance on their own the threat from Russia. Policymakers in Paris should not forget the spectacle of the National Assembly rejecting the European Defence Community in 1954.

The careful balance struck in the UK–French Saint-Malo agreement on European defence, discussed in Chapter 2, remains the best way of reconciling these various approaches. London and Paris both signed up there to the proposition that strengthening European military capabilities would contribute to 'the vitality of a modernised Atlantic Alliance'. They also specified that EU forces would only be used when 'the alliance as a whole was not engaged'. That marked (grudging) French acceptance that for the foreseeable future, the fledgling EU military capacity would be used at the lower end of the military spectrum, for example on missions like peacekeeping, training and disaster relief. That position remains the centre of gravity in the European debate. Macron's much more ambitious agenda for Europe and defence has so far fallen on deaf ears in many European capitals. Britain is now on the outside and has little influence on the direction of EU policy. But it would bring greater honesty and clarity to the debate about NATO's future if the EU accepted that the goal of strategic autonomy was not to dispense with the US as an ally.

Britain would be knocking at an open door with the Biden administration in making the argument that allies have given the US loyal support over the decades, remain the key differentiator between the free world and autocratic regimes and enable the US to get more done in the world by working with its friends. But NATO means less to the young generation than it does to those who remember the Cold War, and adversaries are adept at using disinformation to sow discord and mislead the public. Their job is made easier because politicians across NATO too often fail to make the case for NATO. Polling by King's College London and Ipsos Mori in 2019[6] revealed widespread ignorance about NATO, particularly amongst the young. For example, in the UK, 41 per cent of over-50s knew something about NATO, but that fell to 25 per cent among the under-35s. There needs to be a concerted campaign in all member states to explain NATO's continuing value to a new generation.

The final piece of the jigsaw in the relaunching of NATO would be a clearer strategic purpose around which all member states could rally.[7] That can only be achieved by making NATO more relevant to the most pressing security concerns of its member states. NATO is already doing more to counter Russian adventurism. It now needs to become the forum for coordinating a response to the challenge posed by China to Western security. This would breathe new life into one of the organization's original purposes as the place for consultations about the issues that really matter to the democracies of Europe and North America. It is after all the only forum they have to do so. Such political consultations were systematic during the Cold War. But they have withered away. If NATO ambassadors had been holding confidential debates about their countries' intentions in Syria, the US might have alerted its allies that it was pulling its forces out, and Turkey might have had the confidence to raise the threats it saw from the Kurdish militias in Syria before sending its troops in, not afterwards. NATO would not have been 'brain-dead'.

There is now a clear case for NATO to have a China strategy, which it never needed in the past. China is extending the reach of its military power into NATO's backyard. There have been times in recent years when there were more Chinese warships in the Mediterranean than French. The Chinese are expanding their activity in the Arctic and buying up strategic assets such as the port of Piraeus in Greece. If NATO is now to be a forum to coordinate policies on Asian security issues, then Australia and New Zealand should be at the table. They already have close links with NATO, having fought in the NATO-led coalition in Afghanistan. So should Japan, which provided logistic support to the NATO operation in Afghanistan, and South Korea, which also has a formal security treaty with the US.

The aim would not be to create a 'global NATO' by amending the Treaty. It would be to bring together like-minded countries round the same table to coordinate responses to China's increasingly aggressive behaviour. One of the key issues would be to look ahead and ensure that the West was never again caught in a position of dependence on China for strategic technologies and manufacturing capacity as was the case with Huawei and 5G. This would give the US a stronger incentive to work through NATO in meeting its most pressing national security needs. The US would have to accept in return that the NATO countries who were also members of the EU would have a collective view on some issues – things have moved on since the US could ban any European caucusing before NATO discussions.

NATO matters even more to Britain in the changing geometry of global power. Britain therefore has every incentive to lead a campaign to restore a sense of mutual confidence among member states. The venerable NATO Alliance could be given a new strategic purpose as the place where all America's closest allies gather to discuss the threats that matter most to them, in Asia and the Middle East as well as in Europe, and in space and cyberspace.

Renewing multilateralism

Alongside the established institutions, more informal groups of countries have come and gone as the agenda shifts. In the post-war years, the four allies with responsibilities in Berlin – the US, Britain, France and the Federal Republic of Germany – met discreetly as the Quad for many years and became an inner steering group for the major European security issues throughout the Cold War. Britain later played a key role in organizing a Contact Group involving all the main countries involved in the long crisis in the Balkans during the 1990s. President Giscard of France convened seven of the leading world economies to deal with the repercussions of the 1973 oil crisis. The G7 has continued to meet annually since then. It has been joined since 2009 by a larger G20 including China. This was convened to deal with the financial crash, but following the inexorable law that international groups are easier to create than dissolve, it also continues to hold an unwieldy annual gathering. The changing power dynamics in Asia have brought India, Japan, Australia and the US together to promote an open and peaceful Indo-Pacific region in response to China's aggressive implementation of its Belt and Road infrastructure programme.

In the face of the US retreat from its leadership role, the middle-sized democracies are showing more interest in caucusing to assert the value of international rules and multilateralism. The German foreign minister, Heiko Maas, called in 2019 for an 'alliance of multilateralists', adding that he was working with France and Canada and that 'the alliance should be an open network for all those who value the power of law and who feel bound by a rules-based order so as to cooperate even more closely in international organisations.'[8]

Contributing ideas and political energies to tackle weaknesses in the existing processes is a natural role for Britain to play. It has the attraction for Johnson's government of dovetailing with rhetoric about a new, more distinctive British approach to the world freed from the supposed constraints of EU membership. For some Brexit supporters, the dream is to reconnect with the Anglosphere, for example building on the Five Eyes intelligence community comprising Australia, Canada, New Zealand, the UK and the US. This has always been narrowly focused on the sharing of signals intelligence and should remain so.[9] If the Five

Eyes cooperation was broadened to handle wider political and security issues, there would be a risk that disagreements on these could spill over and cause damage in the intelligence sharing network. The US has already shown that it was willing to use intelligence sharing as a lever over Britain in the case of Huawei.

There is no shortage of ideas for new groups of democracies. Before he became president, Biden committed to calling a global Summit for Democracy with a focus on fighting corruption, defending election security and promoting human rights. The British government took a step in that direction in their capacity as hosts of the G7 group of industrialized countries (Canada, Germany, France, Italy, Japan, UK, US) in 2021, by inviting Australia, India and South Korea to join the meeting. This might develop into a more permanent D-10 arrangement. It would leave gaps: there would for example be no participation from Latin America or Africa. But it would be a real improvement on the G7.

The House of Commons Foreign Affairs Committee summed up the attraction of a more informal approach to multilateralism when it recommended in October 2020 that 'the UK should use its convening power and thought leadership to bring together nimble networks of like-minded nations. . . These coalitions would be open, issue-based, fleet-footed, overlapping, and even temporary.'[10] These groups can play a vital part in re-energizing international cooperation and campaigning for change. But they are not a panacea. Nor can they substitute for treaty-based organizations and alliances that have been built over decades. Informal groupings do not have the strength in depth that come from support structures like international secretariats.

That is a problem that has dogged the G7 and G20. Member states take the chair for a year in rotation. The agenda and the quality of preparation for each meeting varies according to who is in the chair. Meetings tend to end up as talking shops. There is no systematic follow-up. And they are inevitably transactional. They thrive when all the members are benefiting, but they tend to wither when interests diverge. The G20 group of the world's largest economies served a purpose in the immediate aftermath of the financial crash of 2008–9, but the differences on economic policy, between Western countries on the one hand and states like China and Russia on the other, are so wide that its annual summits have become largely ritualistic. Durable multilateral cooperation involves a willingness sometimes to put the interests of other allies first in the knowledge that they will stand by you when you face tough times. That is why NATO has advantages as a forum for detailed work to forge a coordinated China security strategy among America's closest allies. A new grouping of democracies could be the venue for sharing ideas on wider issues of global governance.

The new post-Covid multilateralism will need both the impetus and fresh thinking that new groups of countries can provide, and the capacity of international organizations with their apparatus of staff and budgets to turn ideas into results.

Rethinking the role of armed force

The armed forces have been at the core of Britain's national identity since at least the Napoleonic Wars. Modern British governments have therefore found it very hard to accept that Britain should be anything other than a first-order power across the entire military spectrum. As I was coordinating the 2010 Strategic Defence and Security Review (SDSR), ministers were explicit that the message was to be no strategic shrinkage, even though the Ministry of Defence's commitments were £20 billion more than its budget, and cuts were inevitable. One option to close that gap would have been to decide that the top priority should be defending the UK and its Overseas Territories and fulfilling NATO obligations. Another option would have been to concentrate on the experience gained from the expeditionary operations of the previous two decades, and make that Britain's specialization. But that would have been out of kilter with public opposition to any more foreign adventures. Unsurprisingly, ministers preferred to hedge their bets, and insist that the armed forces should remain capable of doing everything despite cuts in numbers and some capabilities. By the time of the 2015 SDSR, the choice between projecting power and defending the home base was still unresolved. The future military force structure was still based on the requirement to send a large force a long distance into an international conflict.

The decade after 2010 saw the British armed forces re-equip with a formidable array of new equipment. But Britain struggled to keep up with the relentless pace of technological advance led by the US. By 2020, the black hole in the UK defence budget had grown again to some £13 billion. The significant increase in defence spending announced in late 2020 enables ministers to continue for a few more years keeping open all the options for the future role of the armed forces. They can continue to claim that Britain has world-class capabilities in land, sea and air forces and a new capacity to operate in space and in cyberspace, as well as maintaining a nuclear deterrent and increasing investment in research and development. The new spending commitments secure Britain's place as the leading military power in Europe and give it added credibility in Washington and in NATO. But they do not remove the need for longer-term strategic decisions about the future role of military power.

The option of using the armed forces to project Britain's influence globally is maintained by increasing the size of the Royal Navy (this has the double benefit of creating new jobs in naval shipbuilding, and of conjuring up comforting images of Britain's past greatness as a seafaring power). The entry into service of the two new aircraft carriers opens the prospect of occasional sorties to the Indo-Pacific region, although they would need to be supported by ships from other allied countries and carefully protected in times of tension from the risk of long-range anti-ship missiles. The RAF are readily adaptable to operating against different threats, and embracing new technologies, such as unmanned aircraft and new generations of satellites.

The transition from the era of large-scale interventions in other people's conflicts has been slowest and most painful for the Army, and it is here where choices will have to be made in the coming years. Much of the Army's equipment was bought for the wars in Iraq and Afghanistan, and it is still expected to be capable of joining with allies in defence of NATO territory against a well-equipped Russia, or mounting expeditionary operations against less capable nations far from the UK. But the two tasks require different equipment and organization. In the absence of a clear choice between them, the Army is concentrating on investing in new equipment to make individual units and soldiers more lethal, more mobile and more effective by using artificial intelligence and networks of sensors. The implication of this (which is less often spelled out) is that over time the Army will get smaller, substituting technology for size of forces. But adversaries like Russia are investing both in large-scale conventional forces and in the capacity to operate in the ambiguous area below the level of outright conflict using tools such as cyber attacks and disinformation campaigns. Even with a larger defence budget, it will not be possible for Britain to keep open indefinitely all the options for the future role of its armed forces, and particularly the Army. Choices will need to be made on greater specialization, in the closest cooperation with the US and European nations.

———

Despite the rhetoric of the Leave campaign, a policy based on demonstrating independence and turning away from established institutions will not secure the country's key interests. Britain would be better served by putting real effort into adapting the UN as the only truly global body with the legitimacy to tackle future threats to human survival, and NATO as the best forum for responding to the security issues that matter most to the community of Western democracies. New forms of multilateral cooperation will also be needed in the post-pandemic world, and Britain should bring its experience and creativity to bear here as well. A British role at the heart of the new multilateralism should be accompanied by a new and realistic concept of how the armed forces should be used to promote the country's interests and influence.

9

TRADE, VALUES AND THE MERCANTILIST TRAP

The free trade agreement we have to do with the EU
should be one of the easiest in human history.
Liam Fox, International Trade Secretary, 2017[1]

Champion of free trade

Boris Johnson chose the baroque splendours of the Painted Hall at the Old Royal Naval College in Greenwich to make his big pitch on free trade. The date was chosen with care – 3 February 2020, the first working day after Britain left the European Union. So was the setting. The audience assembled under the recently cleaned ceiling painted by Sir James Thornhill over nineteen years starting in 1707, conveniently also the year in which England and Scotland united. The Prime Minister drew the lesson that the successful resolution of this divisive constitutional question opened the way for Britain to experience 'stability and certainty and optimism and an explosion of global trade propelled by new maritime technology'. Sure enough, he predicted that the same would happen after leaving the EU: 'we are re-emerging after decades of hibernation as a campaigner for global free trade.'

In amongst the swashbuckling rhetoric about Britain's glorious free-trading future, Johnson used another word, which attracted less attention. 'The mercantilists', he said, 'are everywhere, the protectionists are gaining ground.' The Prime Minister made clear that he had no intention of joining the ranks of the protectionists. But the implication of his message was that Britain too was embarking on a more mercantilist foreign policy. Not in the original sense of the term as it was used in the seventeenth and eighteenth centuries to refer to the theory that states grew strong by amassing bullion, either by foreign conquest or by rigging the terms of trade.[2] But in the sense that Britain would have to give much greater priority in its foreign policy to its commercial interests, or to use the definition of mercantilist in the Oxford English Dictionary, 'engaged in trade or commerce, mercenary. . . disposed for bargaining'.

There will be plenty of bargaining in the years ahead as Britain learns in the tough school of international trade negotiations. Not only did Johnson's government make 'global Britain' the centrepiece of British foreign policy just as globalization was in full retreat: they cast themselves as the champions of free trade just as the barriers were being thrown up in all directions. Trump made tariff wars a speciality. His campaign against China developed, as we have seen, into a full-scale use of US sanctions to decouple the technology sectors of the two countries. Trump also slapped tariffs on Canadian timber and German cars in the name of national security. Britain was hit with a 25 per cent levy on Scotch whisky as part of a package in retaliation for the sales practices of Airbus in the US. The Covid-19 pandemic accelerated moves away from global free trade as countries imposed controls on the exports of medical equipment, face masks and pharmaceuticals. The public health crisis gave a new priority to self-sufficiency, and its corollary, protectionism. This was not a good time to launch a campaign for new Free Trade Agreements (FTAs).

It was in any case odd for the Prime Minister to present Britain as the global champion of free trade in the same month that his government opened trade negotiations with the EU in which British objectives were to erect new barriers to trade. Britain insisted on leaving the most complete free trade area in the world with its Single Market and Customs Union, and sacrificing frictionless trade access to the vast market on its doorstep, in order to pursue FTAs with countries much further away with whom trade volumes were much lower.

The chosen model for the EU–UK relationship was the EU–Canada agreement, despite the fact that Canada accounts for a far lower share of EU trade than does the UK (around one tenth of the value).[3] It was therefore no surprise that the EU demanded safeguards beyond those in the EU–Canada agreement in return for tariff-free and quota-free access to its market for the vastly greater EU–UK trade flows. They secured what became known as level playing field provisions, enabling them to impose tariffs if the UK tried to gain unfair trade advantages by undercutting EU rules in areas such as environmental standards and employment law.

The Johnson government held out the prospect that Britain would be able to move on briskly from its negotiations with the EU. Instead, there will be a continuous and open-ended process of bargaining, with regular moments of crisis, to take account of changes in regulation, technology and many other factors. That has been the experience of Norway and Switzerland, who have never been members of the EU, but who have constant and sometimes fractious negotiations with Brussels. Ivan Rogers has observed: 'we shall, like an outsized Switzerland, be negotiating on everything – from fish to financial services, from food and farming to fundamental rights and that is just the Fs – for as long as both the UK and EU exist.'[4] That will be the new, scratchy normal in the UK's economic relationship with the EU.

Throughout its time as an EU member, Britain benefited from the expertise of the Commission, which had spent decades leveraging the economic weight of the member states collectively in negotiations with other countries. Outside the EU, Britain is more exposed, more vulnerable to pressure from all sides. It would have been prudent to finalize the future trade arrangements between Britain and the EU before embarking on FTA negotiations with other important markets. Instead, while the fraught negotiations with the EU continued, the British government launched simultaneously into a series of other trade talks. It sought both to prolong the benefits it had enjoyed as a result of the existing EU trade deals with countries like Japan and Canada, and also to negotiate brand-new deals with the US, Australia and others. British ministers signalled in the clearest terms how keen they were to strike these deals as rapidly as possible in order to show that leaving the EU had served some economic purpose. The cold-eyed trade negotiators in other capitals knew well how to exploit the negotiating leverage that handed them.

The hard reality for an economic power the size of Britain is that trade negotiations will come down to a series of choices over how far to meet demands for access to the British market, and in most cases whether to align with regulatory standards set by the EU or the US. These standards are often the main impediment to the free flow of goods and services and therefore at the heart of trade negotiations. While tariffs are mostly of concern to businesses and attract little public attention, standards matter to consumers, and can be politically highly sensitive. Food safety and animal welfare offer the clearest example. In a recent survey by Britain's Food Standards Agency, 68 per cent of those polled were concerned about food standards.[5] British consumers wanted to maintain the EU rules which prevented the import of chlorine-washed chicken or hormone-treated beef. Yet the US insisted repeatedly that one of its top priorities in a US–UK trade agreement would be to remove these restrictions, as well as others such as certifying that animal welfare rules were being met. They saw all these as discriminating against US agricultural products. Another survey conducted by the Institute for Public Policy Research[6] in Britain showed that only 8 per cent of people were willing to see standards compromised for the sake of an agreement with the US. Australia also set as one of its negotiating objectives with Britain the need to 'assess and remove trade-restrictive measures' largely in the area of food safety.

The more British governments choose to move in the direction of US food standards, the more divergence there will be from EU regulations, and the harder it will be for British exporters to access the EU market. While proclaiming the benefits of a trade deal with the US in the years after the Brexit referendum, ministers were unwilling to prepare the public for the difficult decisions that would be needed if one was to be secured. Instead, they pledged that there would be no compromising on the commitment to maintain existing food standards, while confidently predicting that a trade deal with the US would be signed before Trump left office in early 2021. It was no surprise when that deadline was missed. Britain was however able to sign trade deals with Japan and Canada in late 2020. These were symbolically important in showing that Britain outside the EU could pull off trade deals with major economies. But they largely replicated the terms of the existing deals with the EU. In the case of Japan, a British government impact assessment found that of the £15 billion projected boost to trade between Britain and Japan, over 80 per cent of the benefits would go to Japanese exporters.[7] On a trade agreement with the US, official British estimates were that this could increase UK GDP in the long run by between 0.07 and 0.16 per cent depending on the scenario.[8] The combined effect of this and the deals with Japan, Canada and Australia (when that is concluded) would only offset a tiny fraction of the shortfall created by leaving the EU.

Britain will also have to accept norms imposed by more powerful economic actors in the field of data protection. The American approach is essentially to treat data as a commodity, largely owned by the giants of the internet such as Amazon and Google, although greater attention is now being given to the security of data in the light of the confrontation with China. The EU doctrine is to give much greater priority to data privacy. The EU has established a global lead in setting norms for the protection of online data with its General Data Protection Regulation (GDPR). Most US internet giants have adopted the GDPR as their standard for data privacy, as have over 120 governments. Since the exchange of data is a crucial underpinning for businesses as well as security authorities, it will be vital for the UK to meet the requirements of both US and EU data regulators. The problem is that they often disagree. The EU and US spent years of tortuous negotiation to agree arrangements known as the Privacy Shield to allow companies on both sides of the Atlantic to comply with their different data protection regimes when transferring personal data for business purposes. The European Court of Justice then ruled in 2020 that the Privacy Shield arrangement was incompatible with EU law. As and when Washington and Brussels find a new way to ensure that the data keeps flowing, London will have no option but to sign up to what has been agreed. There is no room for a distinctive British approach to this fundamental underpinning of modern life.

Trading values

All British governments like to make ringing statements about their commitment to fundamental values. So it was no surprise when the Foreign Secretary, Dominic Raab, declared in announcing the launch of Britain's Integrated Review of defence and foreign policy: '. . .our guiding lights will remain the values of free trade, democracy, human rights and the international rule of law.' Previous governments found it hard to follow those guiding lights consistently. The 'ethical approach to foreign policy' announced by Robin Cook on taking office as Blair's Foreign Secretary in 1997 did not last long when he discovered that governing involves hard choices, for example on arms sales.

Trade-offs will be inevitable as the government seeks new economic opportunities internationally to make up for the damage from the recession caused by the Covid-19 crisis and the extra hit from leaving the EU. As we have seen, FTAs with other Western countries will do little to close this gap. All this means that British governments will, for the foreseeable future, have to constantly evaluate whether they can afford to antagonize countries offering sorely needed trade or investment opportunities. It was an unrecognized benefit of EU membership that it provided some collective cover for members to stand up to powerful countries on issues of values.

As an EU member, Britain was in a stronger position to hold China to account for its human rights policies knowing that the government in Beijing had to weigh its major economic interests with the EU in calibrating how to react. Cameron crossed a

Chinese red line by meeting the Dalai Lama in London in 2012, in a display of solidarity with the Tibetan people faced with Chinese repression. The Chinese promptly put relations with Britain into the deep freeze, and it took another eighteen months before another senior ministerial meeting. In the meantime, the Chinese conspicuously cultivated French and German leaders to make their point. Nonetheless, the economic impact of that period in cold storage turned out to be minimal. UK–China trade went up in the 2012–14 period. The Chinese had to balance their irritation against their interests in a successful conclusion of an EU–China investment agreement. Being part of the EU gave member states a degree of protective cover that Britain now lacks.

In response to the Chinese government's imposition of a draconian national security law in Hong Kong in 2020, Britain rightly took the bold step of offering up to three million Hong Kong people permanent residence in the UK. It was a powerful gesture of solidarity with Hong Kong. But it was a political measure. Britain is no longer shielded by EU membership. It needs as we have seen to maintain a working trade and investment relationship with China. Beijing is adept at using access to its vast market as an instrument of political leverage.

The case of Norway is instructive. When the Oslo-based Nobel Prize Committee awarded their Peace Prize to Chinese dissident Liu Xiaobo in 2010, China blocked salmon imports from Norway until Norwegian policies at the UN aligned more closely with China. Without the protective cover of EU membership, Norway had little scope to retaliate. Australia is another case in point. When Canberra called for an international investigation into the origins of the Covid-19 outbreak, China retaliated by banning imports of Australian beef, putting taxes on other products and launching an investigation into wine imports. Australia, like

Britain, cannot rely on the economic clout of a wider grouping to deter these coercive Chinese policies.

The British government made the choice not to apply sanctions to individual members of the Chinese security establishment responsible for implementing the repression in Hong Kong. They could have done so using the British version of the US Magnitsky Act, which became law in the UK while the crackdown in Hong Kong was under way. The US legislation, named after a Russian lawyer who died in a Moscow prison after investigating a massive tax fraud, gives the US administration powers to impose an asset freeze and/or visa bans on those suspected of committing human rights abuses. When Raab announced the first measures under the new British Act in July 2020, the targets included organizations and individuals from Russia, Myanmar, North Korea and Saudi Arabia, but not China.

The main motive for passing the UK version of the Magnitsky Act was outrage at the murder of political opponents of the Russian regime, including in the UK, as well as the scale of money laundering in London by Russian criminals. So there was every reason to include Russians on the list. Britain's relationship with Russia was in any case already at rock bottom after the poisoning of the Skripals in Salisbury. Myanmar and North Korea were obvious choices as countries with terrible human rights records and very limited British economic interests.

The inclusion of Saudi Arabian citizens was a different matter. Saudi Arabia is not a significant trading partner for the UK overall, taking some 1.3 per cent of total British exports. But these are very heavily concentrated in the defence sector. The Riyadh government is the single largest buyer of UK arms, with 43 per cent of total arms exports. The market is therefore crucial for British defence companies. This position has been built up over decades of close cooperation on defence and security. Sustaining it depends on confidence that Britain will remain a trusted national security partner, including in difficult times. That has left Britain walking a very narrow line between criticism of Saudi Arabia for its human rights record and maintaining the confidence of the Saudi ruling elite.

The killing of the journalist Jamal Khashoggi in the Saudi Consulate in Istanbul in 2018 made it harder to walk that line. The result was a carefully measured British statement, in line with those from other Western countries, calling for an investigation. Britain's position was even more awkward in the face of the international condemnation of the Saudi military offensive in Yemen which began in 2015, in particular the air strikes involving significant civilian casualties. Claims that British-supplied weapons were used in these strikes made uncomfortable reading for the British government given the country's distinguished record in developing the laws of war. London only agreed to suspend arms exports that could be used for the war in Yemen after losing a court case brought by human rights activists.

The balancing act between economic interests and fundamental values was well illustrated by the way London handled the inclusion of Saudi officials on the Magnitsky list. The Saudi authorities had already accepted responsibility for the Khashoggi murder, and a number of officials had been convicted, some facing the death penalty. It was therefore a relatively low-risk option to include some Saudis implicated in the murder on the British sanctions list. It cannot have been a coincidence that the following day a British minister announced that the suspension of arms sales to Saudi Arabia was being lifted after an investigation had shown that there had been no pattern of Saudi air strikes in

Yemen which breached international law. Britain continued to walk its narrow path.

———

Johnson's aspiration to be a champion of free trade is already bumping up against the hard fact that open markets, like other aspects of globalization, are now under pressure from protectionist forces generated by the return of great power competition and the impact of the pandemic. Each trade agreement will involve difficult choices about how much to concede. Navigating between the EU and US regulations in areas of acuter concern to citizens, from food and pharmaceutical safety to protection of personal data, will be a constant headache. The imperative need for trade deals as part of economic recovery leaves Britain vulnerable to pressure from economic partners and increases the risk of British foreign policy being caught in the mercantilist trap. The Johnson government has already shown its willingness to trade off Britain's centuries-old reputation for upholding the rule of law to meet a narrow and short-term interest; whether Britain's other fundamental values are up for debate is unclear, but entirely possible.

10

HOW FAR OFFSHORE? BRITAIN, EUROPE AND THE INDO-PACIFIC TILT

We do not see situations arising in which the vital interests
of either France or the UK could be threatened without the
vital interests of the other also being threatened.[1]
Joint Declaration by Jacques Chirac and John Major, 1995

Deepening defence ties

The high-water mark in Britain's rapprochement with Europe on defence and security came on 2 November 2010 in another gilded London palace. This time the venue was Lancaster House and the occasion was the signing of two treaties by Cameron and Sarkozy. The momentum which brought these two centre-right leaders together had begun even before Cameron took office in May 2010: Sarkozy had ended more than four decades of France being a semi-detached member of NATO by bringing his country back into the Integrated Military Structure in 2009. Cameron's opposition team had been exploring before the election the possibility of doing more with the French on defence.

As soon as I had set up the new NSC in 2010, I was given the remit to develop some powerful new initiatives to demonstrate that Britain and France, as Europe's two largest military powers, were working closely together. I got down to intensive talks with my two opposite numbers in the Elysée: the veteran diplomat

Jean-David Levitte, who had been a close adviser to three presidents, and General Benoît Puga, the former head of French Military Intelligence and battle-hardened Director of Special Forces, who was then the president's military adviser. It rapidly emerged that both our bosses were keen to work together on improving military capabilities and saving money through joint procurement of weapons and by sharing facilities.

Six months later, the two treaties were ready to sign. The most far-reaching one attracted least notice. It was on the sharing of nuclear weapons facilities – a largely taboo subject between Britain and France up to that point, given the exceptionally close cooperation between the US and the UK on the technology and operation of the nuclear deterrent. Even so, Britain and France had much in common as nuclear powers. Both kept at all times a submarine armed with nuclear warheads carried on ballistic missiles lurking silently on the floor of the ocean, the ultimate reserve of state power if Armageddon ever came. The two countries had similar doctrines on how to turn this formidable capacity into deterrent effect, as the Chirac/Major statement (which has been repeated at regular intervals since then, including in the Lancaster House Treaty) shows.

What Cameron and Sarkozy signed up to at Lancaster House was a remarkable gesture of mutual confidence. They agreed to build a joint facility to simulate the performance of their nuclear warheads without the need for any nuclear explosion (both countries have renounced live nuclear weapon tests). The physics of this required large and eye-wateringly expensive hydrodynamic facilities using radiography to model the performance and safety of the weapons. Rather than each building their own, Britain and France agreed to share a single installation, tucked away in a remote valley at Valduc in Burgundy. Each would have a sovereign area at the site to store and work on the dummy warheads they brought for testing. The Treaty has a life of fifty years and commits France to ensuring unfettered access to the site throughout that time. Cameron took the risk of signing up to this mutual dependency as a way of symbolizing the deep shared interests between the two countries and of saving millions of pounds by not building a duplicate site in Britain.

UK–French nuclear cooperation is therefore as insulated as it is possible to make it from the shifting tides of political relations. Macron confirmed as much in the big set-piece speech on nuclear deterrence which, by tradition, every French president delivers in order to reaffirm the underlying policy and adapt in carefully calibrated ways to the changing threat. Speaking in February 2020, Macron confirmed the unprecedented level of cooperation on nuclear issues between Britain and France, adding: 'We will pursue this with determination, and Brexit makes no difference to that.'[2] He also made an intriguing point aimed at other members of the EU: 'I would like to see a strategic dialogue develop with those of our European partners who are ready to do so on the role of French nuclear deterrence in our collective security.'

The offer was not greeted with enthusiasm around EU capitals. Governments were reluctant to be drawn into the nuclear domain, which France has always jealously guarded. Public opinion in many European countries, especially Germany, was deeply suspicious of nuclear weapons. As a result, there is no prospect of a shared European nuclear deterrent. But if there is one European country which should be discussing nuclear deterrence in a changing world with France, that is Britain. With Russian announcements on the introduction of new nuclear weapons systems, the emergence of North Korea as a nuclear power and the uncertainties about the longer-term US commitment to NATO, there is every reason to deepen the nuclear dialogue between London and Paris. The Valduc initiative showed that this can be done without cutting across operational cooperation with the Americans.

The second Lancaster House Treaty covered two areas. The first was increasing the capacity of the two armed forces to work together, specifically by developing a Combined Joint Expeditionary Force (CJEF) drawn from army, navy and air force units in the two armed forces. As British Ambassador to France, I had the chance to observe several exercises where British and French units trained together, so as to be ready to deploy on combat operation or in a range of other scenarios from disaster relief to peacekeeping under UN, NATO or EU auspices. Many of the highly professional young officers and their troops had a shared background of tough fighting in Afghanistan. They clearly respected each other, enjoyed working together, spoke enough of each other's language to make themselves understood and even ate the same meals. It was a glimpse of what the future of European military cooperation could be, if the politics allowed. The force reached operational readiness in 2020, and is available for deployment at anything up to the level of a brigade if the two countries felt that they had a high enough level of shared national interest to make this the right choice. The CJEF gives both governments a more robust military option than would be available using the structures of European defence.

France has plenty of incentive to work closely with Britain on defence. But political considerations are pulling Macron in the other direction, towards building up European strategic autonomy through the EU. That is very clear in the second area in which the Lancaster House Treaty broke new ground, on closer cooperation between defence industries. The idea was to run joint programmes where the two countries had similar requirements. They could then share the heavy development costs of modern weapons systems, buying greater numbers between them more cheaply and cooperate on winning export customers. Although there was good cooperation on a new generation of missiles, and new mine-hunting capabilities, the high hopes raised by Lancaster House were largely dashed.

The flagship was to have been a new family of large drones, known as the Future Combat Air System, for the post-2030 period. In 2016, the two governments signed an agreement for a consortium led by BAE and Dassault to build a £2 billion demonstrator programme ready for testing in 2025. This never gathered momentum. After Britain's decision to leave the EU, France's attention moved to cooperation with Germany on a new-generation fighter jet. And, in a significant shift, Germany returned the interest. In the past, Germany often bought US military equipment as part of showing that it was a strong supporter of the transatlantic relationship. To show they were also good Europeans, the Germans joined Britain and Italy in producing two generations of fighter jet, the Tornado and Eurofighter Typhoon. France was left to produce its Mirages and Rafales in proud sovereign independence. It was therefore significant that in 2017 Germany opted, for the first time, for a joint project to build a fast jet with France. Britain was left to embark on a separate jet fighter programme with Italy and Sweden, known as Tempest. Europe's defence industry was once again divided into two competing camps, even though it is highly doubtful that there is a large enough market to make two products viable, given that the cost of each high-tech aircraft means that countries are buying far smaller fleets than in the past.

By 2020, ten years on from the Lancaster House Treaties, much of the political energy had gone out of UK–French defence cooperation. Even though it was never directly dependent on Britain's membership of the EU, it became a casualty of the wider breakdown. For all that, France and Britain are the only world-class military powers in Europe with a shared tradition of using their armed forces as a tool of their foreign policy. French political and military leaders are well aware that, in a serious national security crisis, Britain and France are the only two European countries which could provide the backbone of any European military operation that did not involve the Americans.

The high-profile nature of UK–French defence ties since Lancaster House has tended to overshadow UK–German cooperation. But the UK and Germany take a similar approach to the renewed threat from Russia, have similar sized armed forces and defence budgets, and with the end of large-scale military interventions beyond NATO's borders the two countries have more scope for closer cooperation. They are facing the same decisions in many equipment areas. And London and Berlin are leading the way on a NATO initiative involving larger nations helping groups of smaller ones to improve and modernize their armed forces. The difference in the military cultures of the two countries is reflected in the distinct focus of the two groups. The UK is leading a Joint Expeditionary Force (JEF), with contributions from six smaller North European nations: Denmark, Estonia, Latvia, Lithuania, the Netherlands and Norway. The emphasis of this grouping is improving the capacity for operations on NATO territory or beyond, as part of NATO's Readiness Initiative. A parallel German initiative has brought together twenty-one Central and Eastern European nations to improve their capabilities for the large-scale military operations that would be needed to defend NATO territory. UK and German defence policies are more convergent than they have been since the Cold War, and the growth of cooperation between groups of like-minded European countries large and small gives Britain new opportunities to play to its strength as the leading European military power.

Law enforcement and justice

The pragmatism evident in defence cooperation will be equally necessary if Britain and the EU are to preserve anything approaching the intensity of security cooperation between police forces and judicial authorities that exists among EU members. But it will be more difficult to achieve. Unlike the area of defence, which is still largely outside the EU treaties and therefore gives ministers scope to make political decisions on how closely they wish to cooperate with third countries, EU internal security cooperation is based on detailed legal texts.

Since the 2001 terrorist attacks, the EU has developed an elaborate network of capabilities to allow the security authorities to cooperate seamlessly across international borders. The British police, like their counterparts around the EU, relied heavily on access to the real-time information that these EU instruments provide. Large databases of information, covering fingerprints, DNA and criminal records, allow police to check rapidly whether a suspect has come to the attention of law enforcement in EU countries. The second-generation Schengen Information System (SIS II) gives alerts on the movement of suspects, from terrorists to cases of child abduction. It became so central to the work of the UK police that they consulted it 603 million times in 2019. A senior Metropolitan Police Officer told a House of Lords Committee in 2020 that checking a DNA sample taken at a crime scene in the UK with the records of other European countries used to take four months. Using the EU system, it took fifteen minutes. The European Arrest Warrant made the arrest and return of fugitives from justice an automatic process, removing the risk of political considerations holding up decisions.

Only EU members can be full participants in these various networks of cooperation. As part of the Trade and Cooperation Agreement with the EU, the UK negotiated arrangements to have continued access to the information on these databases, but it will no longer have direct, real-time access. As an EU member, the UK played a key role in developing Europol, the EU's law enforcement agency, which facilitates cooperation among police forces. For many years, the Director of Europol was a UK police officer, and the UK was one of the major users of the organization. Now, the UK link is via a liaison officer with limited rights. Across the board, cooperation on law enforcement and justice will be slower and more labour-intensive. As a result, citizens in the UK and EU will be less safe.

Doing the Indo-Pacific tilt

Foreign policy is the area where successive British governments since the 2016 referendum have flagged up their intention to go offshore in pursuit of 'global Britain'. In practice, the UK continued to stay in step with the EU in this area, even as it disengaged from the economic relationship. Cooperation between London, Paris and Berlin (often referred to as the E3) in particular remained close. The three countries continued to lead international efforts to keep the Iran nuclear deal alive through the Trump years. They jointly worked to sustain efforts on climate and world trade in the face of Trump's withdrawal from the global organizations. They opposed his decision to move the US

Embassy in Israel to Jerusalem. All three supported continued sanctions against Russia over Ukraine. Maintaining this degree of alignment will not be a foregone conclusion. Paris and Berlin will be each other's closest partner and will make much of their foreign policy through the EU. It will be up to Britain to make most of the running in the E3, through the power of its ideas and a willingness to show its value as a close partner by sometimes supporting French or German priorities, even when they are not as important to Britain. Relations with Britain will rarely be anyone else's top priority in Europe. That is the lot of the outsider.

Despite the rhetoric of exceptionalism associated with leaving the EU, Britain still looks at the world from a European perspective, and is bound to share many priorities with our geographical neighbours. That does not, however, add up to an eye-catching new national strategy for a British government which has given overriding priority to making a clean break with the EU. So the search has been on for a new concept to give some content to the vague 'global Britain' aspiration. The Foreign Secretary, Dominic Raab, revealed the direction of thinking when he told the House of Commons in September 2020: 'our vision for a truly global Britain will tilt. . . to the Indo-Pacific region.'[3]

There are good reasons for Britain to put more effort into the Asian region where it has long-standing relations with many countries, stemming from a shared history and values. Countries like Australia, New Zealand, Japan, India, Malaysia and Singapore would all welcome in their different ways greater British engagement in their region and its many problems. Britain shares an interest with Asian democracies on promoting human rights, coordinating on sanctions policy and cyber security, and reducing dependence on China by developing new technologies and the supply chains to go with them. But this is a vast geographical area with no overarching multilateral framework for cooperation. All the Asian democracies look first to Washington for their security. For Britain to make any noticeable impact would mean a dramatic shift of diplomatic resources, which would presumably have to come from Europe or other parts of the world. Even if the government were prepared to do that, and to commit to a greater military presence in the region including regular visits from one of the new aircraft carriers, the UK could never be more than a secondary player in Asian security issues.

The Indo-Pacific tilt also has the attraction for the post-Brexit government of implying that it would be a tilt away from Europe. But what would be the opportunity cost? Although many of the world's most dynamic economies are in Asia, almost half Britain's trade is with its European neighbours, and another 15 per cent with the US. Many of the regulatory decisions that will have greatest impact on Britain, in areas such as data protection and environmental and food standards, will be made by the EU. The best opportunity to exercise British influence on these decisions will be at an early stage while they are still being considered in the capitals of all the member states. Many of the most pressing threats to Britain's national security, from Russian adventurism to Islamist terrorism and migration pressures, will continue to come from Europe and its periphery. An Indo-Pacific tilt would also have to be carried out while Britain was simultaneously engaged in a tilt away from China. To many countries in the region (and perhaps to China) it would look as if the UK was stepping up its role in the region in order to confront China. Yet as we have seen, Britain has a strong incentive to maintain functioning trade and investment links with China.

Pursuing an active foreign policy in Europe and its surrounding areas and also in the Asia-Pacific are not mutually exclusive.

Both are important to UK prosperity and security. But strategy involves choosing. Political, diplomatic and military resources for influencing abroad are finite. Making it a priority to do more across the breadth of Asia would inevitably mean doing less elsewhere, including in Europe. A tilt to the Indo-Pacific is a slogan not a strategy. It does not match closely enough the pattern of Britain's vital interests to become the basis for a durable national strategy.

11

CONCLUSION

*It would help us get a little way on the road if we had
a clearer idea of where we wanted to go.*
Harold Macmillan, 1961[1]

The ravages of Covid-19 changed the world and profoundly affected the way nations think about their security. There is a monumental task ahead to restore economic life and find new ways of living together under the continuing shadow of the virus. It may be true that nothing will ever be the same again. But history suggests otherwise. After the turmoil of the First World War and then the upheaval of the 1918 pandemic, it took only two decades before the world slid back into another cataclysmic war. This book has argued that the much more successful effort to create stability after the Second World War is still relevant to today's challenges.

As the world recovers from the latest catastrophe, there is a lot we can learn from the great surge of institution-building in the decade after 1945, distilling the experience of those who had lived through wars and economic depression, and how the organizations they created grappled with the problems of international security. The post-war system was showing the strain of coping with the changing balance of power even before the pandemic struck. The maelstrom since then has laid bare serious weaknesses in the international organizations just as it did in national governments. But it has also highlighted new forms of cooperation, particularly the worldwide network of collaboration between scientists, researchers and pharmaceutical companies to develop vaccines in response to Covid-19. The case for this cooperation to be mirrored by a new multilateralism amongst governments in the post-pandemic world is compelling. The system we inherited from the 1940s needs deep reform. But it still has strengths which could never be replicated and which will still be valuable in the future. In trying to build new forms of international cooperation, the old adage about not throwing the baby out with the bathwater still applies.

What lessons can we draw from the effort to create a comprehensive international system for the post-war world? Two of the key points are apparent in that phrase. First, it was a genuinely comprehensive approach to the issue of security, based on a coherent vision of the future which British statesmen had helped to shape. The UN Charter sought to outlaw war and regulate behaviour between states, and to create in the Security Council a body with real enforcement powers. The IMF aimed to improve international financial coordination, the GATT to reduce barriers to trade, and the World Bank and Marshall fund to rebuild shattered countries and address the most pressing human security issues. NATO was established as a community of democracies to promote their values as well as a military alliance to defend them. Six European countries embarked on a project, which became the EU, to integrate their economies and so to make war between them impossible.

Over the decades, the sense of a holistic approach to security has been lost as each organization has pursued its own course with minimal coordination. We have seen how, throughout the Cold

War, NATO and the EEC cohabited in Brussels as if they were on different planets. The international community struggled to produce a coherent response to the 2008 financial crash, which is why the G20 group of states was created to give leadership. The world trading system became bogged down, fractured into a series of regional deals. Western countries were slow to recognise their dependence on China for high-technology manufacturing and the security implications of that. The response to the pandemic has required governments to make intensely difficult trade-offs between public health and economic imperatives.

Second, the system put in place in the 1940s was a decisive rejection of zero-sum nationalism in favour of international cooperation. It was only possible because the US as the world's hyper-power in 1945 decided to follow Roosevelt's logic – and some persuasive British ideas – in agreeing to be bound by the same set of rules as all other countries. They then went a step further by accepting the case made so powerfully by Bevin to commit to the transatlantic alliance in NATO, recognizing the logic that the US needed allies in order to make the world safe for America. But there were only brief periods when genuine cooperation on security was possible. Inevitably, the Security Council was stalemated by disagreements among permanent members and increasingly unrepresentative of the real power balance in the world. The Iraq effect pushed the US into a long retreat from international leadership and emboldened nationalist powers like Russia to defy the international rule book in their turn. There was no strategic unity among NATO members as the US turned towards a bilateral confrontation with China.

The pandemic has added to the existing pressures on the international system a new imperative for national self-reliance. In a human health crisis, citizens will always look in the first place to their own governments to protect them. Public health systems are national, and scarcities of life-saving medical equipment and drugs inevitably led countries to compete with each other to secure vital supplies. The effect in the early stages was to drive countries apart. By putting the spotlight on resilience against future disruptive shocks, the Covid-19 crisis may mark a turning point away from the globalization of the manufacturing industry and the worldwide dependence on China this has created. But economic recovery will need more, not less, international trade and investment. The resumption of international travel will need harmonization of health requirements for travellers.

Adapting to these new realities will need new forms of cooperation between governments. On trade, it will reinforce the move towards regional agreements among countries with similar interests. New coalitions of like-minded countries will form, as they have always done, to campaign for reforms and raise consciousness about specific problems. But they will not have the institutional underpinning to turn these campaigns into durable international mechanisms. Nor will they be able to replicate the globality of the UN and the legitimacy that comes with it. From that point of view, the network of UN specialized agencies is unique. Agencies like the WHO urgently need reform, including more secure arrangements for funding, so that they can be freed from suspicions of clientism towards their largest donors. They need to be better managed and more efficient, and to work more effectively together to give advance warning of potential new risks. But they are a legacy of the post-war system which it would be impossible to replicate in today's polarized world and are therefore worth remodelling as part of the new multilateralism.

The pandemic also makes a new approach to national security essential, giving an even more prominent place to resilience against disruptive threats to human life and modern society. Here, the experience of Britain's 2010 and 2015 National Security Strategies is telling. These documents flagged up these risks, including pandemics, as among the most important facing the country. Contingency plans were made, but not followed through into spending hard cash on more intensive care wards and stockpiles of essential equipment. Real resilience will need a change of behaviour by governments towards providing spare capacity in areas of critical national infrastructure and accepting the additional cost as a necessary insurance premium in an unpredictable world.

That in turn highlights the problem that, during the long period of strategic stability since 1945, Western governments lost the art of strategic thinking. The intense pressures on modern democratic government mean that the short term and urgent get all the attention, squeezing out the long term. We have seen that politicians can often regard strategic thinking as a waste of time when keeping their job depends on handling the crisis of the moment, and when trying to look ahead seems pointless given the scale and pace of disruptive change. The information revolution, fuelled by the power of social media, has had a profound effect on policymaking. It has raised the tempo of the political cycle to the point where decisions are often rushed and ill thought out. Britain's recent history is littered with examples of where momentous judgements were made by instinct or conviction but without systematic thought about longer-term consequences – from Blair's decision to join George W. Bush in invading Iraq to Cameron's gamble of a referendum on the EU and the chaotic handling of Britain's departure from the EU by the May and Johnson governments.

The pandemic has also shown the fragility of the modern interconnected world. Climate change poses an existential threat at least as serious in the longer term, and modern societies could be brought to a halt at any time by a collapse of digital systems. The pandemic will ensure massive investments in public health in the UK, just as the intelligence agencies had money thrown at them for a decade after 9/11. But will it unlock investment to anticipate other shocks, for example, better protection for critical national infrastructure from attacks of all kinds, or a concerted drive to reduce carbon emissions? In my experience, the likelihood is that democratic governments will return to dealing with the immediate demands of their electorates rather than making the mental leap of preparing for the next disruptive shock.

All of this is relevant to the hard choices Britain faces in defining a new post-EU national strategy while coping with a changing international landscape. Cadogan's influence on the Atlantic and UN Charters showed the power ideas have to shape international affairs. It was also a reminder that if good ideas are to have a durable effect, they need to be amplified by support from powerful friends and reflected in the structures of international cooperation. Britain's influence in the world was at a high point in the 1940s. It has declined a long way since then, much further than many British people realize. The country's political system was torn apart by the issue of Europe, leading to a new relationship with the EU defying any rational calculation of the country's longer-term economic and security interests and leaving it vulnerable to pressures of all kinds from larger economic and political blocs. The lacklustre response to the pandemic resulted in deep damage to the economy and to the fabric of society. The precious asset of Britain's reputation as a country whose word could be trusted and that respected the rule of law was tarnished by the threat to break international law.

The combination of leaving the EU and the human and economic impact of the pandemic have hit Britain hard. The country badly needs a new national strategy. Giving top priority to an independent role based on a notion of British exceptionalism would lead to marginalization. An effective strategy will need to be based on realism about the country's weight in the world, and a shrewd targeting of finite resources to achieve the changes that matter most. It should reflect the reality that Britain's best way of exercising global influence will be to mobilize its powers of example, ideas and persuasion. The armed forces are a huge national asset. But the Army in particular is still coming to grips with the shift from large expeditionary operations in failed states to facing well-equipped adversaries like Russia, adept at exploiting the grey area just below open conflict. Britain still lacks a clear concept of how the armed forces should be used to promote the country's influence.

Britain should be a creative force in organizing new forms of multilateral cooperation where the Covid crisis has shown gaps in the existing system. New groups of like-minded democracies could prove useful. But nimble networks are limited in what they can achieve. They can generate ideas, but it is then up to each individual member to take them forward. There tends to be no continuity from one meeting to another, and no capacity to translate ideas into action. For that, the existing international organizations with their staff and their budgets still have their value. The global membership of the UN and its specialized agencies could never be replicated in our fractured world, and could play a key role in improving resilience. Britain still needs NATO, both for its collective defence and the consultation forum it provides. That should be expanded to cover Asian security, with America's Asian allies around the table.

Britain's urgent need for new free trade agreements to aid economic recovery means that the choice has already been made in practice – even if it is not avowed in public – to pay whatever price is necessary to secure agreements with larger economic partners. The UK will inevitably have to accept standards set by others ranging from data protection to food and pharmaceutical safety, and deals on market access of greater benefit to those who can exercise the strongest leverage. The choice for British governments will often boil down to how honest to be with the public about the concessions they have been obliged to make by the hard logic of trade negotiations. They will also have to choose whether to own up to the fact that, outside the EU, Britain is more exposed to the mercantilist trap, and that it will on occasion have to give lower priority to a values-based foreign policy championing human rights and fundamental freedoms when that could put at risk trade or investment.

America's confrontation with China is a generational struggle. Where Britain positions itself within that polarity will be its most significant national security decision in the coming years – and one fraught with difficulty, as the Huawei episode has already shown. The US is Britain's largest trade and investment partner. But British trade with China will continue to grow, especially if China continues to recover from the global economic crisis more quickly than other markets. Britain could never be neutral between the US and China. The defence and security relationship with Washington will remain crucially important, even though London's value to Washington has diminished as a result of leaving the EU. On national security, Britain's unequivocal choice has to be to stand with the US, including in a drive to develop strategic technologies of the future to avoid dependence on China. But on global governance, the balance looks different. Britain's interest is not in systematic confrontation but in Chinese engagement in a reformed international system, including new organizations that will give China greater influence within a set of rules. China and the West are strategic rivals but economic partners. Encouraging China to play its full role in tackling global problems like climate change without cutting across the underlying US–UK national security partnership will be a difficult balancing act.

The EU, like other international organizations, was sidelined in the early stages of the pandemic, as its members scrambled to protect their own publics. But by the end of 2020, the EU had agreed a €750 billion economic recovery programme, involving the richer members agreeing for the first time to issue common EU debt in order to support those facing the greatest pressures. Covid-19 had the effect of pushing the EU towards greater integration, as member states realized the value of solidarity in times of economic turmoil. That effect is unlikely to last. Wide variations in economic performance in an EU of twenty-seven countries make a single, Eurozone-based, set of economic rules even harder to sustain. The Eastern European members of the EU have brought different social models and, in the case of Hungary, a different attitude towards some of the EU's founding values. In order to survive, the EU will have to become a looser structure over time, more tolerant of diversity. The kind of EU, in other words, which the UK long advocated when it was a member.

Britain's departure from the EU makes a period of political estrangement inevitable. Dismantling the web of links based on shared EU membership, and finding new ways of working as economic partners at arm's length, will take years. For as long as Britain pursues a distant economic relationship, defence and security relations will be weakened. Citizens in the UK and EU are less safe as a result of the loss of real-time access to the networks and databases which underpin EU cooperation on justice and security. The momentum of UK–French defence cooperation has ebbed as France is caught between promoting European strategic autonomy based on the EU and holding on to the practical benefits of cooperation with Britain's armed forces. UK–German defence cooperation has been slow to take off, and is constrained by the growth of Franco-German defence industrial links. It is a similar story on foreign-policy coordination between London, Paris and Berlin. That has benefits for all three, but the hard reality is that France and Germany will always put their shared EU interests first.

A new national strategy is an integral part of adapting to life outside the EU. It could make one further important contribution to navigating the difficult decisions which lie ahead. That is to tackle the wide gap between Britain's real influence in the world and the public perception – assiduously cultivated by campaigners for Britain to leave the EU – that the country could somehow return to its glorious past as a great power. For advocates of this approach, the notion of British exceptionalism offered a route map through the post-Brexit world. This nostalgic fantasy was already making realistic policymaking more difficult; the pandemic makes it even more urgent to use a new strategy to argue the case that Britain's strength in the world will rest in the future, as it did in the past, on international cooperation with friends and allies.

If a national strategy is to influence how a wide range of citizens think about Britain's role and purpose in the world, then government documents like the Integrated Review are only a point of departure. A much wider national conversation is needed so that members of the public can influence the gradual development of a more modern and inclusive national story than the sepia-tinged memories of former glories that many in my generation have tended to cling to. It means, crucially, involving the younger generation, whose lives will be most affected by the strategy decisions made now. Such a national conversation is possible in the age of the internet.

The French government have made them something of a speciality. After six months of the *gilets jaunes* (yellow jackets) protests against social and economic conditions in France during 2018, Macron launched a *grand débat national* in January 2019, grouping possible areas for reform into four broad themes. Over the following three months, town halls across France opened 16,000 *cahiers de doléances* (books for citizens to record their grievances, a phrase resonant with echoes of the French Revolution). Over ten thousand local meetings were organized and two million online contributions analysed. The results were fed into a series of national conferences, and brought together into a 1,500-page synthesis. Debates were held in the National Assembly and the Senate. Macron announced his conclusions in a long press conference on 25 April 2019. He judiciously mixed some contrition for his arrogance, some tax cuts and pension increases, and some reform of the French political system including more use of referendums. It fell far short of answering all the grievances behind the protests, but it did enough to convince enough of the French people that the government had listened for the protests to peter out.

The themes of the *grand débat* were very wide-ranging. A more tightly focused French model was the Citizens' Convention on climate change, made up of 150 participants chosen at random and tasked with formulating proposals to meet the target of reducing greenhouse gas emissions by 40 per cent. The Convention met for six months from October 2019, supported by (and perhaps guided by) a government-appointed committee of experts. Once again, the government made a careful selection of which of their conclusions to adopt, doing enough to show that the exercise had been worthwhile.

The concept of a Convention has deep roots in French history going back to the revolution. A rather more peaceful precedent is the Irish tradition of public consultation. In 2012, a Constitutional Convention was established by the government in Dublin with sixty-six randomly chosen citizens and thirty-three representatives of the political parties. It spent fifteen months considering seven constitutional issues chosen by the government and two more of its own choosing. The government accepted some of their recommendations, rejected others and asked for further consultations on the remainder. A Citizens' Assembly was set up in 2016 with a similar pattern of membership to consider seven constitutional issues, including highly contentious ones such as abortion. The Assembly's conclusions on this were widely seen as paving the way for the 2019 law decriminalizing abortion in Ireland.

On a much smaller scale, citizens' assemblies to discuss specific issues have been used by national and local government in many countries. The first UK-wide citizens' assembly on climate change was convened by six parliamentary committees in 2019 to consider how Britain could reach its target of net zero greenhouse gas emissions by 2050. The assembly involved around 100 people and met over six weekends before publishing a report in September 2020. A national conversation to develop a new sense of Britain's international role would need to be broader and more sustained than that, taking the government's Integrated Review document as a point of departure.

Changing deeply rooted assumptions, and bringing a wide range of people to accept a new narrative as representing modern

Britain, is a long-term process. It will require a government willing to listen to other viewpoints and take account of them in its own thinking. There was no sign of that in the years after the Brexit decision. The determination to pursue a distant relationship with the EU has increased the risk of Scottish independence or the unification of the two parts of Ireland, or both. The rump state of England and Wales would then join the ranks of other European countries whose glorious past was remembered mainly through their splendid public monuments and the contents of their art galleries. A status equivalent to the Netherlands, Spain or Portugal would make England's absence from the EU even more anomalous, especially if Scotland proceeded to join in its own right. That is the level of uncertainty which faces the Union of Great Britain and Northern Ireland in the decade to come.

Britain's hardest choice is, therefore, also the simplest: to accept reality. Britain is and will remain a European power, international by instinct and history, by the structure of its economy and the global spread of its people. But a European power nonetheless, intimately bound up with what happens on the continent, as it has been throughout history. The 2016 decision to leave the EU was the result of a particular set of economic, social and political circumstances. There were sincere and deeply held convictions on both sides of the argument, but very few undisputed facts on which to make a decision with such long-term consequences. It was not based on any clear vision of an alternative basis for Britain's prosperity or role in the world. The much vaunted 'taking back control' has already turned out to be meaningless in the face of a pandemic that respected no borders. The same will be true of future disruptive shocks. On top of this, Britain chose to leave the EU just as the changing geometry of power fractured the world into competing blocs. The deepening competition between the world's two largest economies makes it a perilous time for the UK to leave the protective cover provided by the EU and forge out alone. China has developed a speciality in turning access to its market on and off as a tool of its foreign policy. 'The strong do what they can,' Thuycidides quoted the Athenians as saying to the Melians, 'and the weak suffer what they must.'[2] Middle-sized and smaller independent nations are finding that the decisions that affect them most are ones they have least control over. In that world, the system of international rules is crucial, yet the British government has damaged its credibility in defending those rules by casting doubt on its commitment to international law. Much of Britain's influence in the world depends on its soft power, especially at a time when public opinion is very wary of using the armed forces in an assertive way as an instrument of foreign policy. Yet the Johnson government has chosen to increase spending massively on military equipment and to sharply reduce the development budget. We are still some way from a coherent national strategy.

Building a new future outside the EU will change Britain in the decades ahead in ways that cannot yet be foreseen. The risk is that it will make the country both poorer and more introspective. The details of how and why it happened will gradually fade into history. But the consequences will remain. One of the most striking features of the 2016 referendum was the scale of opposition by young people to Britain's departure: estimates suggest that over 70 per cent of eighteen- to twenty-four-year-olds voted to remain.[3] That generation will be denied opportunities enjoyed by their contemporaries around Europe, such as the life-changing chance for students to live and study in other EU countries under the Erasmus programme or, for those starting a business, the advantages of unfettered access to a single market of 450 million people. They will arrive in power in politics and business knowing that they have been denied precious benefits without any compensating advantages from Britain's new 'independent' status. They will not be encumbered by nostalgic fantasies about a return to a golden age of British greatness. I am confident that they will find creative ways for a changed Britain more at ease with itself to rebuild a close partnership with a changing European Union.

For centuries, Britain has reconciled its position as a European power with its interests around the world. The next generation will need to match Alec Cadogan's combination of vision and pragmatism in making the hard choices involved in that double destiny.

NOTES

Introduction

1 There are many ways of measuring the relative size of economies. The IMF's *World Economic Outlook for October 2020* shows that China's share of global Gross Domestic Product in Purchasing Power Parity (PPP) terms was 18.6 per cent, while the US share was 16 per cent. But in current US dollars, the US economy is around a third bigger than China's. For India, the OECD's *Long Term Forecast 2018* projected that India's economy would overtake the US's in PPP terms in the mid-2030s.

2 To differentiate the two Presidents Bush, I refer to the father, who was President from 1989 to 1993, as George H. W. Bush, and the son, President from 2001 to 2009, as George W. Bush.

3 Prime Minister Tony Blair, speech in Chicago, 24 April 1999.

4 UK's Record on pandemic deaths, *British Medical Journal*, 4 September 2020.

5 *GDP: International Comparisons*, House of Commons Library, 22 December 2020.

1. Imagining the Post-War Order

1 Address to University of California Convocation, 13 May 1954.

2 Sir Alexander Cadogan, 'Atlantic Meeting Aug 41', unpublished memoir written in 1962, Cadogan Papers, Churchill College, Cambridge, AC/AD7/2.

3 Woodrow Wilson, speech to US Congress, 8 January 1918.

4 The story of the Kellogg–Briand (or Paris Peace) Pact is recounted in Oona A. Hathaway and Scott Shapiro, *The Internationalists*, London, Allen Lane, 2017.

5 Elizabeth Borgwardt, *A New Deal for the World: America's Vision for Human Rights*, Cambridge, MA, Harvard University Press, 2005, p. 6. The book gives a detailed account of the US intellectual background to the Atlantic Charter, and its later influence on international human rights policy.

6 Ibid., p. 20.

7 Andrew Roberts, in his biography of Churchill, remarks that 'it was astonishing that so committed an imperialist as Churchill could have put his name to Article three, but such was the imperative of establishing common purpose with the United States.' *Churchill: Walking with Destiny*, London, Allen Lane, 2018, p. 676.

8 The quotation is taken from an account of the dinner by Roosevelt's son Elliott, who was present. He had a habit of putting words into people's mouths, so the Churchillian tones may have been enhanced, but the general drift is plausible.

9 Reflecting in retirement on the Atlantic Charter, Cadogan commented: 'It was a most remarkable and significant document for the President of the United States, then not at war, to have sponsored.' Memoir, op. cit.

10 For an account of the Charter's reception in the UK, see David Reynolds, 'The Atlantic "Flop": British Foreign Policy and the Churchill-Roosevelt Meeting of August 1941', in Douglas Brinkley and David R. Facey-Crowther (eds.), *The Atlantic Charter*, New York, St. Martin's Press, 1994.

11 Borgwardt, op. cit., p. 4.

12 Farewell Address to the US Congress, 19 September 1796.

2. Managing an Alliance of Unequals

1 On the *Today Show*, February 1998, in the context of enforcing the no-fly zone in Iraq, quoted in Micah Zenko, 'The Myth of the Indispensable Nation', *Foreign Policy*, 6 November 2014.

2 Sir Clive Rose, British Diplomatic Oral History database, Churchill College, Cambridge, https://www.chu.cam.ac.uk/ media/uploads/files/Rose.pdf (accessed 18 December 2020).

3 Andrew Adonis, *Ernest Bevin: Labour's Churchill*, London, Biteback 2020, Chapter 9.

4 *Review of Soviet Policy*, 5 January 1948, Documents in British Policy Overseas (DBPO), Series 1, vol. X, no. 9.

5 *The First Aim of British Foreign Policy*, 4 January 1948, DBPO Series 1, vol. X, no. 7. The strength of Bevin's conviction about the wider ethical value of NATO comes out in a radio address he gave shortly after signing the Treaty: '[NATO] is an endeavour to express on paper the underlying determination to preserve our way of life – freedom of the press, freedom of religion, and the rights and liberty of the individual.'

6 Telegram from Bevin to Lord Inverchapel, Washington, 10 March 1948, DBPO Series 1, vol. X, no. 63.

7 For a recent example, see Robert B. Zoellick, *America in the World: A History of US Diplomacy and Foreign Policy*, New York, Twelve Books, 2020, pp. 288–90.

8 *A Report to the National Security Council - NSC 68*, 12 April 1950, https://www.trumanlibrary.gov/library/research-files/ report-national-security-council-nsc-68?documentid=NA&page number=1 (accessed 18 December 2020).

9 Quoted in Kori Schake, 'Trump Doesn't Need a Second "Solarium"', *Atlantic*, 30 October 2018, https://www.theatlantic. com/ideas/archive/2018/10/what-eisenhower-could-teach- trump-about-strategy/574261/ (accessed 18 December 2020).

10 They took away very different lessons from the experience, Britain redoubling its commitment to the special relationship, and France vowing to maintain its strategic autonomy.

11 Belgium, the Federal Republic of Germany, France, Italy, Luxembourg and the Netherlands.

12 *A National Security Strategy of Engagement and Enlargement*, July 1994, p. 21.

13 That was not to be Milošević's fate. He was indicted for war crimes by the International Criminal Tribunal for Yugoslavia in The Hague and died in jail there in 2006.

14 'The Doctrine of International Community', speech to the Economic Club of Chicago, 24 April 1999.

15 R. C. Eichenberg, 'US Public Opinion and the Use of Military Force', *International Security*, vol. 30, no. 1 (Summer 2005).

3. Rethinking the Use of Force

1 UN Secretary-General, press conference, 24 February 1998, on the issue of bringing Saddam Hussein to comply with Iraq's UN obligations.

2 Germany was serving a term as a non-permanent member of the Security Council at this time.

3 Interview for the *Frontline* programme, PBS, 17 May 2016.

4 Fuller accounts of this sequence of meetings from a British perspective are given by Jack Straw in *Last Man Standing*, London, Macmillan, 2012, Chapter 16; and Sir Jeremy Greenstock in *Iraq: The Cost of War*, London, Penguin, 2016, Chapters 9 and 10.

5 ICM/*Guardian* poll, 16 March 2003.

6 'Iraq, the Last Pre-War Polls', Ipsos MORI, 21 March 2003.

7 The town was granted Royal patronage in 2011 in recognition of its role in military repatriations.

8 Peter D. Feaver and Christopher Gelpi, *Choosing Your Battles: American Civil-Military Relations and the Use of Force*, Princeton, Princeton University Press, 2004, p. 97.

9 David Cameron, *For the Record*, London, William Collins, 2019, p. 276.

10 This phrase was first quoted in a long article by Ryan Lizza in the *New Yorker*, 'The Consequentialist: How the Arab Spring Remade Obama's Foreign Policy', 25 April 2011. It was widely adopted as a pithy summary of Obama's foreign policy.

11 Quoted in Jeffrey Goldberg, 'The Obama Doctrine', *Atlantic*, April 2016.

12 David Cameron, op. cit., p. 450.

13 Jeffrey Goldberg, op. cit.

14 All quotations taken from House of Commons *Hansard*, 29 August 2013.

15 Jeffrey Goldberg, op. cit.

16 'Defence Expenditure of NATO countries 2013–20', NATO Public Diplomacy Division press release, 21 October 2020. There are several ways of counting defence budgets and some show lower spending than the NATO definition used here.

17 France and Britain plan to spend roughly similar amounts in the coming years. France committed to spend a total of €198 billion in the four years 2019–23: French Embassy press release, 9 February 2018. The UK plans to spend £190 billion total in the four years 2021–5: Prime Minister's statement to the House of Commons on the Integrated Review, 19 November 2020.

18 In 2020, it was still functioning, at the much-reduced scale of 600 personnel.

19 Trineke Palm and Ben Crum, 'Military Operations and the EU's Identity as an Intergovernmental Security Actor', *European Security*, vol. 28 (2019), issue 4.

20 David Cameron, op. cit., p. 276.

21 See, for example, Elliot A. Cohen, *Supreme Command: Soldiers, Statesmen, and Leadership in Wartime*, New York, Simon & Schuster, 2002.

22 The Council of Europe has grown to forty-seven countries from every corner of Europe, including Russia and Turkey.

23 It is often confused with the European Court of Justice applying EU law from its HQ in Luxembourg.

24 These paragraphs draw on the analysis in T. Tugendhat et al., *Clearing the Fog of War*, Policy Exchange, 2015.

25 The case known as *Al-Skeini* mainly concerned the deaths of five claimants in Basra, and whether or not the UK had a duty under the ECHR to investigate those deaths. This was a test for the applicability of the ECHR to the British Army's occupation of Basra. (2011) 53 EHRR 18.

26 In particular Smith v MOD (2013).

27 Evidence to the House of Commons Defence Select Committee, 2014.

28 *Al-Jedda* (2011) 53 EHRR 23.

29 Tugendhat et al., op. cit.

30 'Professor Phil Shiner and the Solicitors Disciplinary Tribunal', statement by the Solicitors Regulation Authority, 2 February 2017.

31 'IHAT to close at the end of June', statement by the Ministry of Defence, London, 5 April 2017.

32 Overseas Operations (Service Personnel and Veterans) Bill, 2020.

33 'Iraq War damaged Britain's reputation in the world', Ipsos MORI, 19 March 2013.

34 Joseph Nye, *The Future of Power*, New York, PublicAffairs, 2011, p. 31.

4. Picking the Right Threats

1 Written in 1902. Text fitted to music previously composed by Elgar.

2 *Detainee Mistreatment and Rendition 2001–10*, Intelligence and Security Committee of Parliament, London, 2018, HC1113, p. 4.

3 *Report of the Official Account of the Bombings in London on 7 July 2005*, House of Commons, 11 May 2006, HC 1087, para. 75.

4 Cabinet Office, London, March 2018.

5 'Terrorism in the EU: terror attacks, deaths and arrests in 2019', European Parliament News, updated 3 November 2020, https://www.europarl.europa.eu/news/en/headlines/security/2018 0703STO07125/terrorism-in-the-eu-terror-attacks-deaths-and-arrests-in-2019 (accessed 12 January 2021).

6 *Underlying Cause of Death 1999–2017*, Centers for Disease Control and Prevention, wonder.cdc.gov (accessed 23 December 2020).

7 *A Strong Britain in an Age of Uncertainty*, HM Government Cmnd 7953, October 2010.

8 *Securing Britain in an Age of Uncertainty*, HM Government Cmnd 7948, October 2010.

9 Ciaran Martin, 'Cyber weapons are called viruses for a reason: Statecraft and security in the digital age', inaugural lecture, King's College London, November 2020.

10 Tony Blair, *A Journey*, London, Hutchinson, 2010, p. 293.

11 Cmnd 7953, p. 31.

12 UK Influenza Pandemic Preparedness Strategy 2011, Department of Health, 10 November 2011, https://assets.publishing.service.gov.uk/government/uploads/system/uploads/attachment_data/file/213717/dh_131040.pdf (accessed 28 December 2020).

13 'Exclusive: Video shows key UK official in 2016 anticipating "a pandemic that killed a lot of people"', *New Statesman*, 9 May 2020.

5. Reviving the Lost Art of Strategy

1 Testimony before Congress, quoted in Coral Bell, *The Conventions of Crisis*, Oxford, Oxford University Press, 1971, p. 2.

2 Andrew Roberts, *Masters and Commanders*, London, Allen Lane, 2008, p. 574.

3 John Lewis Gaddis, *On Grand Strategy*, London, Allen Lane, 2018.

4 B. H. Liddell Hart, *Strategy*, London, Faber and Faber, 1967, p. 322.

5 Hal Brands, *The Promise and Pitfalls of Grand Strategy*, Strategic Studies Institute, US Army War College, 2012.

6 Lawrence Freedman, *Strategy: A History*, Oxford, Oxford University Press, 2013, p. xii.

7 Prime Minister's covering minute to the Cabinet Paper *Future Policy Study*, 29 February 1960, National Archives, London, CAB/129/100.

8 Ibid.

9 Peter Hennessy agrees from his much broader perspective as a historian of post-war British governments. In his survey of the 1950s *Having It So Good* (London, Allen Lane, 2006, p. 576), he comments: 'The Future Policy Study outstrips in its detail and reach any comparable review of the UK's place and prospects in the world I have ever encountered.'

10 Peter Hennessy, *Winds of Change: Britain in the Early Sixties*, London, Allen Lane, 2019, Chapter 2.

11 All the quotations in this passage are taken from vol. 3 of Charles Moore's biography of Thatcher, *Herself Alone*, London, Allen Lane, 2019, Chapter 15.

12 Ibid., p. 478.

13 'Reforming the National Security Council' in *America's National Security Architecture: Rebuilding the Foundation*, The Aspen Institute, 2016, p. 107.

14 *Who Does National Strategy?*, report by Public Administration Select Committee, House of Commons, 2010.

15 *National Security Strategy and Strategic Defence and Security Review 2015*, Cmnd 9161.

16 Charles D. Freilich, *Israeli National Security: A New Strategy for an Era of Change*, Oxford, Oxford University Press, 2018, p. 7.

17 Isabel Hardman, *Why We Get the Wrong Politicians*, London, Atlantic Books, 2018.

18 Quoted in Daniel Deudney and G. John Ikenberry, 'Liberal World: The Resilient Order', *Foreign Affairs*, July/August 2018.

19 Tony Blair, op. cit., p. 345.

20 Evidence to the Chilcot Inquiry, 29 June 2010.

21 David Cameron, op. cit., p. 398.

22 Kate Fall, *The Gatekeeper*, London, Harper Collins, 2010, p. 131.

23 Ivan Rogers, *9 Lessons in Brexit*, London, Short Books, 2019.

24 'Economic cost of Brexit laid bare in OBR forecasts', *Financial Times*, 11 March 2020.

25 Tom McTague, 'How the Pandemic Revealed Britain's National Illness', *Atlantic*, 12 August 2020.

6. Finding the Power to Influence

1 Northern Ireland Protocol: Legal Obligations, *Hansard*, 8 September 2020, vol. 679, col. 509.

2 Cmnd 9161, paras. 1.10–1.15.

3 One simple illustration of this assertion is the number of overseas tourist visits. In 2015, the last year for which data is available, Britons made 65.72 million visits, almost exactly one visit per head of the population that year. Only Germans travelled more often, on a per capita basis. *Yearbook of Tourism Statistics 2018*, World Tourism Organization.

4 *Global Brit*, Institute of Public Policy Research, 2010.

5 David Reynolds, *Island Stories: Britain and Its History in the Age of Brexit*, London, William Collins, 2019, p. 5.

6 *Exploring foreign investment: where does the UK invest, and who invests in the UK?*, Office of National Statistics, 1 November 2018. The document does not appear to have been updated since then.

7 Studies of trade flows have consistently shown that trade roughly halves as the distance between countries doubles.

8 *Soft Power 30 index*, Portland Communications, available at https://softpower30.com (accessed 30 December 2020).

9 A Deltapoll UK survey of British adults carried out in December 2019 and January 2020.

10 Chapter 39 of the Magna Carta. An English translation can be found at https://www.bl.uk/magna-carta/articles/magna-carta-english-translation (accessed 13 January 2021).

11 Boris Johnson, Conservative Party Conference speech, 6 October 2020, available at https://www.conservatives.com/news/conservative-party-conference-2020-speeches (accessed 30 December 2020).

12 *Group of Governmental Experts on Developments in the Field of Information and Telecommunicaions in the Context of International Security*, UN Document A/68/98, 24 June 2013.

13 UN Document A/70/74, 22 July 2015.

14 But the 2019 *Lowy Global Diplomacy Index* finds that the UK ranks eleventh in its league table comparing the diplomatic networks of sixty-one major countries. See https://globaldiplomacyindex.lowyinstitute.org (accessed 30 December 2020).

15 Figures from 'Key Takeaways from the Foreign Office's 2018–19 Departmental Accounts', British Foreign Policy Group, 15 July 2019, https://bfpg.co.uk/2019/07 (accessed 30 December 2020).

16 'Global Britain', Prime Minister's Statement to the House of Commons, 16 June 2020.

7. Triangle of Tension: Britain, America and China

1 Quoted in James Kynge, 'China, Hong Kong and the world: Is Xi Jinping overplaying his hand?', *Financial Times*, 10 July 2020.

2 Prime Minister's Questions, House of Commons, 10 June 2020.

3 'Full remarks: Joe Biden campaigns in Dallas', *Citizens' Voice*, 24 October 2020.

4 Graham Allison, *Destined for War: Can China and America Escape Thucydides's Trap?*, London, Scribe, 2017.

5 Kori Schake, *Safe Passage: The Transition from British to American Hegemony*, Cambridge, MA, Harvard University Press, 2017, p. 271.

6 'China Could Overtake the US as the World's Largest Economy by 2024', World Economic Forum, 20 July 2020.

7 Charter of the United Nations, 1945, Article 2, para. 7.

8 'Why Trump no longer talks about the trade deficit with China', *Financial Times*, 1 September 2020.

9 'Apple's China iPhone sales jump 225% in the second quarter', CNBC, 28 July 2020.

10 The NCSC website (https://ncsc.gov.uk) is a good example of the openness on the part of the formerly secretive intelligence community.

11 Reported in the *Guardian*, 13 January 2020.

12 *GDP: International Comparisons*, House of Commons Library research briefing, 13 November 2020.

8. The International System and the Lure of the New

1 *A brave new Britain? The future of the UK's international policy*, House of Commons, HC380, 22 October 2020.

2 Boris Johnson, speech, 24 July 2019.

3 'WHO struggles to prove itself in the face of Covid-19', *Financial Times*, 13 July 2020.

4 Merkel made the comment after a bruising encounter with Trump at the G7 summit in Munich on 28 May 2017.

5 Quoted in *Zeitenwende: German Foreign and Security Policy*, Munich Security Conference Report, 2020.

6 *Public Perceptions of NATO*, Policy Institute, King's College London, December 2019.

7 A large number of specific recommendations for strengthening the political dimension of NATO are set out in *NATO 2030: United for a New Era*, the report of a Reflection Group appointed by the NATO Secretary-General published on 25 November 2020. https://www.nato.int/nato_static_fl2014/assets/pdf/2020/12/pdf/201201-Reflection-Group-Final-Report-Uni.pdf (accessed 13 January 2021).

8 Interview in *Der Spiegel Online*, 11 January 2019.

9 Five Eyes grew out of UK–US signals intelligence cooperation during the war. This was formalized in the 1946 UK–USA Treaty, which the other three countries joined in the following years.

10 House of Commons Report HC380.

9. Trade, Values and the Mercantilist Trap

1 Speaking as International Trade Secretary to BBC Radio 4 *Today* programme, 20 July 2017.

2 A practice much criticized by Adam Smith in his *Wealth of Nations* of 1776. See Jesse Norman, *Adam Smith: What He Thought and Why It Matters*, London, Allen Lane 2018.

3 The 2019 figures were: UK imports from the EU £372 billion; UK exports to the EU £300 billion; Canadian imports from the EU €38 billion; Canadian exports to the EU €21 billion.

4 Sir Ivan Rogers, speech at University College London, 22 January 2019.

5 James Kane, *Trade and Regulation After Brexit*, Institute for Government, August 2020, p. 6.

6 Ibid., p. 6.

7 'Labour hits at Truss over benefits from Japan deal', *Financial Times*, 29 October 2020.

8 *UK–US Free Trade Agreement*, Department for International trade, London, 2020.

10. How Far Offshore? Britain, Europe and the Indo-Pacific Tilt

1 UK–French Joint Statement on Nuclear Cooperation, 30 October 1995.

2 Speech by the President of the French Republic, l'Ecole de Guerre, Paris, 7 February 2020.

3 House of Commons, 2 September 2020, *Hansard*, col. 201.

11. Conclusion

1 Grand Design memorandum, January 1961.

2 *Melian Dialogues* 89. Johanna Hanink, in *How to Think About War: An Ancient Guide to Foreign Policy*, Princeton, Princeton University Press, 2019, gives a more accurate, if less pithy, translation: 'Those in positions of power do what their power permits, while the weak have no choice but to accept it.'

3 'Just over 70% of 18 to 24-year-olds who voted in the referendum backed Remain, four major academic and commercial polls conducted shortly after the ballot agree, with just under 30% backing Leave.' Sir John Curtice, Professor of Politics, Strathclyde University, quoted in 'How young and old would vote on Brexit now', BBC News, 9 August 2018.

Acknowledgements

1 Virginia Woolf, *Roger Fry*, Peregrine Books, 1979, p. 108.

ACKNOWLEDGEMENTS

Virginia Woolf commented that 'a first book is apt to lay a load upon a writer's vivacity.'[1] It has certainly been a test of stamina for a former civil servant trained to reduce any problem to two pages at most. I have needed a lot of support and advice over the last three years, and I am hugely grateful to the many people who gave their help so generously.

My colleague on the cross benches of the House of Lords Peter Hennessy first prompted me to write about my forty years of experience in national security. His deep knowledge of recent British political history and unrivalled capacity to bring it to life with just the right anecdote have been an inspiration. Peter put me in touch with Stuart Proffitt at Allen Lane, who could not have been kinder or more patient in coaching a new author to turn his jumble of ideas into a coherent argument. Although he did not in the end publish the result, I owe him a lot.

I also benefited greatly in the early stages from the advice and encouragement of John Bew when he was Professor in History and Foreign Policy in the War Studies Department of King's College London, before he had the rare opportunity to practise in the 10 Downing Street Policy Unit the grand strategy which he had taught with such conviction as an academic. John also put me in touch with one of his PhD students, Andrew Ehrhardt. Andrew and I found that we shared a fascination with the careers of two remarkable British diplomats, Sir Alexander Cadogan and Sir (later Lord) Gladwyn Jebb. Andrew was endlessly willing to pursue research queries, and invited me to discuss my emerging thinking at the Centre for Grand Strategy, which he organized. I hope his unpublished thesis on 'The British Foreign Office and the Creation of the United Nations Organisation' will soon see the light of day as a book.

I am very grateful to John Gearson, Professor of National Security Studies and now Vice Dean at King's College, for inviting me to become a Visiting Professor at King's, thereby enabling me to test and sharpen my ideas in discussions over several years with students on National Security Studies, and Diplomacy and Foreign Policy MA courses. Each of these sessions gave me new insights. Warm thanks to Maeve Ryan, Nina Musgrave and Joseph Devanny for welcoming me into their classes.

David Reynolds, Emeritus Professor of International History at Cambridge, generously agreed to read my manuscript, and gave me many useful insights. The Royal United Services Institute (of which I am a trustee) kindly organized a seminar to help me think more clearly about future defence policy options.

I have learned an enormous amount throughout my career from colleagues in the British Civil Service and counterparts in other capitals. I am particularly grateful to Sir Mark Lyall Grant, Sir Simon Fraser, Sir David Omand and John Casson for reading my work at various stages, suggesting improvements and pointing out flaws. Among my US friends, Kori Schake read an early version of the manuscript when she was Deputy Director-General of the International Institute for Strategic Studies in London, and gave me stimulating advice. Nicholas Burns, my counterpart when we were both Permanent Representative to NATO, invited me to graze all too briefly at the intellectual banquet at the Belfer Center at Harvard, where he was Professor of the Practice of Diplomacy.

My agent, Toby Mundy, inspired and encouraged me, and came up with the book's title. James Pulford and his team at

Atlantic Books embraced the project with enthusiasm, and worked with patience and meticulous professionalism to shape my material into a book, despite the odd working conditions imposed by the pandemic.

Ian Rowley twice subjected the manuscript to eagle-eyed scrutiny, with very beneficial results.

All have helped deepen my analysis and sharpen my arguments; the judgements are mine alone.

But my most heartfelt gratitude goes to Suzanne, my wife and best friend, who believed in this project from the outset, read and improved every draft, and has been my keenest editorial adviser throughout the journey.

Peter Ricketts, January 2021

INDEX